The Story of the FBI

J. EDGAR HOOVER
DIRECTOR, FEDERAL BUREAU OF INVESTIGATION

THE OFFICIAL PICTURE HISTORY OF THE

FEDERAL BUREAU OF INVESTIGATION

The Story
of the FBI

by the EDITORS
of LOOK (periodical)

with an introduction by J. EDGAR HOOVER

NEW AND REVISED EDITION

E. P. DUTTON & CO., INC. NEW YORK

Contents

IN MEMORY OF
SPECIAL AGENTS
OF THE
FEDERAL BUREAU
OF INVESTIGATION
WHO HAVE GIVEN THEIR LIVES
IN LINE OF DUTY

EDWIN C. SHANAHAN	OCT. 11, 1925
PAUL E. REYNOLDS	AUG. 9, 1929
ALBERT L. INGLE	NOV. 24, 1931
RAYMOND J. CAFFREY	JUNE 17, 1933
RUPERT V. SURRATT	OCT. 8, 1933
W. CARTER BAUM	APRIL 22, 1934
HERMAN E. HOLLIS	NOV. 27, 1934
SAMUEL P. COWLEY	NOV. 28, 1934
NELSON B. KLEIN	AUG. 16, 1935
WIMBERLY W. BAKER	APR. 17, 1937
TRUETT E. ROWE	JUNE 1, 1937
WILLIAM R. RAMSEY	MAY 3, 1938
HUBERT J. TREACY, JR.	MARCH 13, 1942
P. E. FOXWORTH	JAN. 15, 1943
HAROLD D. HABERFELD	JAN. 15, 1943
J. CORDES DELWORTH	DEC. 3, 1945
JOSEPH J. BROCK	JULY 26, 1952
J. BRADY MURPHY	SEPT. 26, 1953

IT WAS a pleasure to cooperate with, and lend all possible assistance to, the Editors of *Look* Magazine in the compilation and publication of *The Story of the FBI*. For the first time the full story of the Federal Bureau of Investigation has been told pictorially. Ours is a "WE" organization and to the faithful men and women of the FBI goes most of the credit for our accomplishments over the years, both in peace and in war.

J. EDGAR HOOVER
Director
Federal Bureau of Investigation

RANDOLPH.
1789-94

Introduction

By J. Edgar Hoover

THE Federal Bureau of Investigation is the investigative arm of the United States Department of Justice, which is headed by the Attorney General, chief legal officer of the United States. The functions of the FBI are twofold. First, as a fact-finding agency, it investigates violations of Federal laws and presents its findings to the Attorney General, his assistants and the United States Attorneys, who decide whether those involved are to be brought to trial. Second, as a service agency, the FBI aids law enforcement in identification, technical, training and record matters.

The FBI is as zealous to guard the civil liberties of those accused as it is to bring about their conviction. We report only what we find, without color or deductive evaluation. We collect and present the facts, favorable or unfavorable.

In the event prosecution is authorized, then a judge or a jury passes upon the guilt or innocence of the accused. In no instance does the FBI file a complaint against a person on its own initiative, without first presenting the facts to a United States Attorney and securing his authorization.

Federal law enforcement in the United States dates back to September 24, 1789, when the office of the Attorney General of the United States was created by Act of Congress and Edmund Randolph was appointed the first Attorney General by President Washington. Nearly a hundred years later, on June 22, 1870, the Department of Justice was created by Congress. On March 3, 1871, $50,000 was appropriated for "Detection and Prosecution of

9

Crimes"; it was the first money appropriated in the United States for such a purpose. The Attorney General at that time appointed an Agent, later called a Special Agent, who was paid from this appropriation. This Special Agent conducted special investigations for the Attorney General.

In 1907, the Attorney General called to the attention of Congress that the Department of Justice possessed no permanent investigative force under its immediate control. The Sundry Civil Service Bill passed on May 27, 1908, prevented Secret Service employees from accepting investigative assignments with the Department of Justice, as had been customary up to that time. This action was the real inception of the Federal Bureau of Investigation as we know it today.

On July 26 of the same year, Attorney General Charles J. Bonaparte issued an order that all investigative matters in the Department of Justice should be referred to the "Chief Examiner," who would designate appropriate Special Agents. A limited number of investigators were subsequently appointed.

In 1909, the Attorney General suggested to President William Howard Taft that all "detective duties" directly connected with actual or contemplated Federal civil or criminal proceedings should be entrusted to a force organized as Agents of the Bureau of Investigation. Accordingly, on March 16, 1909, Attorney General George W. Wickersham issued an order establishing the Bureau of Investigation of the Department of Justice, thus confirming Attorney General Bonaparte's previous action. The Chief Examiner's title was changed to "Chief of the Bureau of Investigation."

The small organization grew gradually. The White Slave Traffic Act passed on June 25, 1910, was one of the early criminal statutes in the Bureau's jurisdiction.

THE FBI IN THE FIRST WORLD WAR

The year 1914 marked the beginning of world war. Violations of neutrality laws demanded investigative attention, and numerous reports were received concerning alleged illegal activities of German agents. Although these reports were often false, nevertheless extensive investigation was required. In 1916, international disputes arose along the Mexican border which demanded that further facts be obtained by investigations of the Bureau.

10

On April 6, 1917, the United States declared the existence of a state of war, and thereafter it became necessary to arrest and intern dangerous enemy aliens, to enforce the Espionage Act, the Selective Service Act, and to investigate charges of war profiteering, frauds against the Government, obstruction of recruiting, violations by camp followers, and indications of subversive activities by alien enemies.

Immediately before the outbreak of war, preparations had been made for the arrest and internment of enemy aliens. After formal recognition of the state of war and the almost unanimous approval by Congress, a Presidential Proclamation was issued setting forth regulations under which enemy aliens were to be interned on issuance of a Presidential warrant. Sixty-three arrests and internments were immediately accomplished. Long lists of German sympathizers were classified and the most dangerous of the enemy aliens were soon interned. On June 30, 1917, 295 arrests and internments had been made.

War industry was practically defenseless against sabotage before the entry of the United States into the first World War. A number of intelligence agencies acting without coordination or training were unable to prevent sabotage. While good results were obtained

The disastrous explosion on Black Tom Island in 1916 pointed up sabotage dangers before U.S. defense agencies were coordinated.

eventually, obviously the witch hunts, dragnet raids, and mob hysteria which prevailed in that era sometimes violated the very purpose of the war "to make the world safe for democracy."

Prior to 1917 ships in American harbors were damaged by bombs, bridges were blown up, and ammunition worth millions of dollars was destroyed. The effects of sabotage literally reached from war to war, for claimants spent twenty years and thousands of dollars in litigation costs in attempting to place blame for the destruction.

Among the earliest sabotage acts was the blasting of the Canadian side of the International Bridge at Vanceboro, Maine, on February 2, 1915, by Werner Horn, who had seen ten years of service in the German Army. He was sentenced in June, 1917, to serve eighteen months in a Federal prison and to pay a fine of $1,000.

The city of New York was rocked by the greatest explosion in its history on July 30, 1916, when more than two million pounds of explosives stored on Black Tom Island in New York harbor blew up. Some of the blasts were heard in Philadelphia, nearly a hundred miles away.

Still another powerful explosion occurred on January 11, 1917, when approximately half a million three-inch shells were discharged in the shell assembling plant of the Canadian Car and Foundry Company near Kingsland, New Jersey.

But despite such catastrophes in the first World War, there was no centralization of national defense activities in the FBI, as was the case more than two decades later.

The year 1919 signalized an outbreak of subversive activity on the part of foreign and native radical elements, a movement which had been rigorously suppressed by statutory enactment and public opinion during the war. The Deportation Statute had been passed on October 16, 1918. On October 1 of the following year, a division within the Bureau of Investigation was created to cope with the marked growth of radicalism and the dissemination of anarchistic propaganda. At that time I was assigned as a Special Assistant to the Attorney General and was detailed to the prosecution of the deportation proceedings. The raids were carried on by the Bureau of Investigation, although I had no responsibility for them. Emma Goldman and Alexander Berkman were arrested in November, 1919. Early in January, 1920, Ludwig Martins and Gregory Weinstein, active revolutionists both here and abroad, were deported.

The history of the first World War did much to make obvious the need for freedom from political hamstringing in law enforcement and for carefully chosen and trained personnel. These general observations were made known to Attorney General Harlan Fiske Stone, later Chief Justice of the United States, some years after 1918.

FOUNDATION OF THE FBI OF TODAY

I was designated Acting Director of the Bureau by Attorney General Stone on May 10, 1924, and on May 27 issued a circular order instructing all investigative activity of the Bureau to be confined to certain violations over which the Department of Justice and the Bureau of Investigation had jurisdiction. Mr. Stone approved my recommendations for the far-reaching changes in the structure and policies of the Bureau of Investigation, and the foundation of the FBI of today was the result.

Instructions went out that no appointments were to be made of Special Agents unless appointees had been graduated from some recognized law school or college. Age limits for new employees were set at 25 to 35 years for Special Agents and 25 to 40 years for Special Accountants, with preference in appointment for Special Agents being given to qualified lawyers. No longer was political connection to be given consideration, other than that afforded to endorsements of any kind.

A personnel reduction of 61 was effected during the last few months of the 1924 fiscal year. Regular inspections of all Field Offices were begun; these offices were reorganized, and the policy of promotion predicated upon efficiency alone was inaugurated.

One of the most significant steps taken by the FBI at the time of its reorganization was the creation of a nation-wide identification file in Washington, D. C. As far back as September 24, 1904, the warden of the United States Penitentiary at Leavenworth, Kansas, had requested the authority of the Attorney General to make expenditures for equipment to take fingerprints of Federal prisoners. This authority was granted on November 2 of the same year.

Many years before, in 1896, the International Association of Chiefs of Police had established a bureau in Chicago (later moved to Washington, D. C.) which was known as the National Bureau of Criminal Identification, for the purpose of compiling Bertillon records. As the members of the association discontinued the use of Bertillon measurements and began adopting the fingerprint system, the National Bureau of Criminal Identification gradually built up a valuable collection of fingerprint records. In response to growing and insistent demand by police officials throughout the country for one system of co-operation on a national scale, the Identification Division of the FBI was created in 1924 through a consolidation of the files of the National Bureau of Criminal Identification and the Leavenworth Penitentiary Bureau.

Among the early investigative activities of the fledgling Bureau were the famous Osage Indian murder case investigation in 1923 and the conviction of Dr. Frederick Cook in 1923 on a charge of using the mails to defraud in connection with oil promotion schemes. In 1925, the Bureau conducted a successful investigation of the wreck of the airship *Shenandoah*. This same year witnessed the second conviction of Gaston B. Means on a charge of conspiracy to bribe a former Attorney General and other Government officials.

In October, 1926, a special Fugitive Unit of the Bureau was created and during that year Gerald Chapman, who later was executed in Connecticut for killing a policeman, and Martin J. Durkin, murderer of Special Agent E. C. Shanahan of the Bureau in 1925, were apprehended. In 1927, the notorious Ray and Roy DeAutremont, who had been fugitives from justice since October, 1923, were taken into custody.

One of the landmarks in FBI history occurred in 1930 when Congress authorized the FBI to collect and compile uniform crime statistics for the entire United States. The first monthly bulletin was published in August, 1930, and contained data voluntarily submitted by police and other enforcement officials. It was the beginning of our Uniform Crime Reports bulletin, as we know it today. During 1953, 5,728 agencies contributed crime reports in connection with the project.

In 1930, there also occurred the identification of Jake Fleagle, one of the most important in the annals of fingerprinting. He and three others had entered the First National Bank of Lamar, Colorado, on May 23, 1928, and brandishing guns, ordered all present to hold up their hands. The robbers took some $200,000, and shot the bank president and his son. A doctor called to dress the wounds of one of the injured bandits was blindfolded, shot and pushed over

14

a cliff in his car.

Local officers found the wrecked automobile of the physician and located on it one latent finger impression. Photographs of this were submitted to the Identification Division of the FBI and all fingerprint experts were instructed to impress the pattern indelibly upon their memories. More than a year later, the arrest record of one William Harrison Holden was submitted by the sheriff at Stockton, California. Albert Ground, a fingerprint technician, in reviewing the record, identified one fingerprint with that found on the car of the doctor in the Fleagle case. Holden was none other than Jake Fleagle and his identification led ultimately to the complete solution of the case and the exoneration of four suspects who had been charged with the crime in state court. Jake Fleagle himself was killed while resisting arrest; his three companions received death sentences.

On September 1, 1932, what is today the FBI Laboratory was established in one room with a single microscope. The Laboratory has been a bulwark in the fight against crime, and last year 126,518 examinations involving 112,675 specimens of evidence were made.

HOW THE G-MEN GOT THEIR NAME

Early on the morning of September 26, 1933, a small group of men surrounded a house in Memphis, Tennessee. In the house was George "Machine-Gun" Kelly, late of Leavenworth Penitentiary, and wanted by the FBI for kidnaping. For two months we had trailed the gangster and his wife, Kathryn Kelly. Quickly the men of the FBI, accompanied by local law enforcement officers, closed in around the house and entered.

Ordered to surrender, Kelly stood cowering in a corner. His heavy face twitched. Reaching trembling hands toward the ceiling he whimpered, "Don't shoot, G-Men; don't shoot!"

That was the beginning of a new name for FBI Agents. By the time Kelly had been convicted and had received his sentence of life imprisonment, the new nickname, an abbreviation of "Government Men," had spread through the underworld.

"Machine-Gun" Kelly was a product of the wave of lawlessness which swept over the nation in the early thirties. Kidnaping, mur-

Building occupied by the U. S. Department of Justice until 1899 (left), and that used prior to Department's move in 1934.

Except for Identification Division and training establishments, national FBI facilities and offices are housed in the Department of Justice Building.

16

der, bank robbery, and many other crimes of violence occurred daily. Dangerous outlaws enlisted the petty thief, the small-fry hoodlum, and the ex-convict to form powerful gangs. Professional killers were hired to eliminate honest law enforcement officers, civic-minded citizens, and members of rival gangs.

To check this wave of lawlessness, Congress swiftly passed many new laws to increase the authority of the Federal Bureau of Investigation. In 1932, the Federal Kidnaping Statute, making it a crime to take kidnaped persons from one state to another, was passed. During the following year, the FBI solved every kidnaping case referred to it.

Next came the Federal Extortion Act, by which the writer of a threatening letter could be put in prison for as long as 20 years and be fined $5,000.

Bank robberies by notorious gangsters were met with the Federal Bank Robbery Act, which now extends its protection to National banks, Federal Reserve banks, *and banks or banking-type institutions whose deposits are insured by the Federal Government.*

By 1934 Congress had finished the task of building the FBI into the general investigative agency of the Federal Government. Since then additional duties have been assigned by laws designed better to protect the citizens of the United States. Now the FBI is responsible for the investigation of violations of more than 130 Federal statutes ranging from bankruptcy to treason.

The Department of Justice moved into its new building on Pennsylvania Avenue, between Ninth and Tenth Streets, in 1934. President Franklin D. Roosevelt and other high officials of the Government were present at the impressive dedication ceremonies on October 25. Here FBI operations throughout the United States and its Territorial Possessions are co-ordinated.

Making certain that the FBI functions effectively is my responsibility. FBI headquarters is made up of seven divisions. Division One, the Identification Division, handles fingerprint matters. Training and Inspection in the FBI are the responsibility of Division Two. Division Three is administrative. Records, communications, and the compilations of crime statistics are handled by Division Four. Division Five, the Domestic Intelligence Division, and Division Six, the General Investigative Division, are responsible for the supervision of cases coming within the FBI's Investigative jurisdiction. The FBI Laboratory, Division Seven, provides the FBI and

17

other law enforcement agencies with scientific aids in crime detection.

An Associate Director, two Assistants to the Director, and six Assistant Directors carefully systemize the work of the Special Agent Supervisors and clerical employees in the several divisions.

The efficient operation of FBI headquarters is reflected in every Bureau Field Office, headed by a Special Agent in Charge. In addition, each Field Office has one or more Assistant Special Agents in Charge, and a staff of Special Agents and clerical employees. Each Field Division is charged with the duty of properly investigating all FBI matters within its territory.

The highly geared operations of the FBI are closely knit by telephone, teletype, and radio. Centered in Washington, D. C., the FBI's huge communications system makes possible immediate FBI action in any corner of the nation. In addition, telephone and teletype connections between Field Offices assist in co-ordinating the work of such offices.

Franklin D. Roosevelt (lower left) and other dignitaries attended dedication of new Department of Justice Building in October, 1934.

In the fiscal year ending July 1, 1935, there were 3,717 convictions in cases investigated by the FBI. The total savings in recoveries effected was $38,481,686.17, while the entire cost of operating the Bureau was only $4,626,508. Outstanding investigations successfully concluded during the year pertained to the Dillinger gang, the Kansas City massacre, and the Charles F. Urschel, George Weyerhaeuser, Lindbergh and Bremer kidnapings.

On July 29, 1935, the first session of the FBI National Academy opened at the Bureau for the study by law enforcement officers of scientific and practical law enforcement methods.

During the following year, 1936, from May 1 to May 11, Alvin Karpis, Harry Campbell, William Dainard and Thomas H. Robinson, fugitives in three major kidnapings and objects of nation-wide search for more than a year, were taken into custody.

Strict economy in operations has always been impressed upon all personnel of the FBI. During May, 1938, however, because of unforeseen and costly added investigative burdens, it was necessary to place half of the investigative personnel on enforced leave during May and June. Before the end of the period, however, a deficiency appropriation was voted by Congress to enable the Bureau to carry on its work. In many instances it has been possible for the FBI to turn back into the Treasury substantial portions of its appropriation which were unexpended. For example, in 1943 there was returned unexpended $912,063. In 1944, the unexpended amount was $1,534,721, while in 1945 it was $6,810,458, and in 1946 it was $1,256,593.

THE FBI AGAINST THE AXIS

Early in the growth and development of the FBI after 1924, information concerning subversive organizations and individuals whose basic interests were motivated from abroad came to the attention of the Bureau. Our widespread network picked up bits of information from Europe, South America and the Orient. Pieced together, the reports verified suspicions that the Axis powers were preparing to divide the world.

In a Long Island aircraft factory, a tall, grim-faced man stole blueprints of new bombing planes. Key designs of new American fighting ships disappeared. In Madison Square Garden the growing strength of the Nazi-inspired, German-American Bund impressively revealed itself as 18,000 Bundists and their friends saluted with upraised arms, and "heiled" Hitler to the roll of drums and the parading of swastika flags.

In this crisis the FBI went to work. At a time when most people assumed that the Federal Bureau of Investigation was interested only in cleaning up the remnants of the criminal underworld, Special Agents were making preparations for the new underground fight.

Those were days when America in general was not war-conscious. The armament program for national defense was merely a "security measure." The nation was emerging from an economic depression, and its mind was on other things. For months FBI Agents worked hard to flank the forces of enemy intelligence. It was not enough to know there were spies operating in the United States; sufficient evidence had to be gathered to convict them in an American court.

Important information came to light. There was a fantastic Nazi plot to steal the secret plans for the defense of the East Coast of the United States by luring a high-ranking American Army officer to a New York hotel room, overpowering him and seizing the papers. And then on Saint Valentine's Day, 1938, a spy made an attempt to secure 35 blank American passports by impersonating an official in the State Department. That spy was Guenther Gustave Maria Rumrich, and his arrest followed immediately.

Rumrich was among the first enemy spies to be arrested in this country. Then red-haired Johanna Hoffman; slender, thin-faced Otto Voss, and a fellow traveler, Erich Glaser, were apprehended. The American public was startled. So was German Intelligence. Fourteen agents affiliated with the German diplomatic service fled the country. In Germany, Nazi spies operating as messengers to the United States were removed from ships before they sailed. Fearful as to just how much the FBI knew, Nazi Intelligence officers at Bremen were confused. Almost immediately the German-American Bund prepared to go underground.

Brought to trial, Rumrich, Hoffman, Voss and Glaser were convicted. But the penalties were light. This was "peacetime" espionage, and the sentences for all four spies totaled 14 years.

It was soon apparent that the most effective counterespionage was to check the movements of prying enemy agents. Little was accomplished by arresting spies after their damaging work had been done. As later developments proved, it was necessary to know the innermost workings of enemy espionage—the extent of their networks, their plans for causing damage in our country through sabotage, their interest in certain highly confidential military information. Enemy espionage not only required detection, it had to be prevented. German agents were being skillfully trained and a wave of sabotage was expected. Comprehensive plans were drawn, outlining the anticipated war functions of the FBI.

THE FBI'S HEAVIEST RESPONSIBILITY

In June, 1939, the President issued a directive placing full responsibility for all espionage, counterespionage and sabotage matters in the hands of the FBI and the Army and Navy Intelligence Services. The directors of each of these services were to function as a coordinating committee and, by agreement, the FBI was to handle civilian suspects, the Army and Navy their own personnel. A few days after Hitler's legions poured into Poland, the President issued another directive on September 6, 1939, calling upon all law enforcement agencies to report directly to the FBI any information pertaining to espionage, counterespionage, subversive activities, and violations of our neutrality.

By these Presidential orders the FBI was given the heaviest responsibility in its history—the job of protecting the internal security of the United States against foreign enemies. It was not necessary to build a new agency. The techniques of advanced scientific crime detection that had proved indispensable in conquering home-bred banditry were now set to work uncovering the enemy. Data in the extensive Identification Division fingerprint files infallibly pointed out the true identities of suspects. Special Agent personnel necessarily increased from 851 men to more than six times that number. Total personnel—clerical, laboratory and Special Agent—reached an allotted 14,300.

The burden of training all employees, new and old, in wartime duties fell upon the instructors of the FBI Academy. Congress appropriated funds for the construction of an FBI barracks and for various firearms training ranges at the United States Marine Corps Reservation at Quantico, Virginia. During the height of the recruitment program, newly appointed Special Agents went into training each Monday morning and worked daily from 9 A.M. to 9 P.M. for four months before their assignment to Field Offices.

21

At the peak of the wartime expansion program, up to 1,000 employees were in training at the same time. Each new Special Agent received more than 1,000 hours of lecture instruction—the equivalent of two years of college work. Already qualified as a lawyer or accountant, or college-trained in foreign languages, each trainee also qualified as an expert in firearms as well as becoming a skilled investigator. A daily class in athletic training kept trainees in trim. Judo and various defensive tactics, which had been taught to the early United States Marine Corps Commando groups by FBI instructors, were also taught each class of new men.

Qualifications for all personnel remained at high standards. In-service courses for experienced Agents continued and they were returned to Washington for instruction in new wartime duties. Special courses were provided for all Special Agents, instructors and technicians in handling investigations of major cases and in making surveys of industrial plant facilities.

The receipt of complaints in national defense matters reached flood proportions as the German military machine won victory after victory. In the five-year period preceding 1938, the FBI investigated an average of 35 espionage matters each year. In the fiscal year 1938, 250 such complaints were handled by the FBI, while in the fiscal year 1939, a total of 1,651 matters concerning internal security were received for investigation. With the outbreak of war in Europe and the Presidential proclamations of September, 1939, establishing a limited emergency, this type of work deluged our Field Offices. On one day alone in May of 1940, a total of 2,871 complaints was received.

New Field Offices were opened in Honolulu, Puerto Rico and Alaska. It was also necessary to increase the number of offices within the continental United States, to bring men and materials nearer to centers of population and areas where a concentration of investigative personnel was deemed advisable. Ten FBI offices were opened. Every major city was covered either by a Field Office with headquarters at that locale or by a number of Resident Special Agents operating out of one of the near-by Field Offices. At Washington a Security Division was created at FBI headquarters, under the supervision of an Assistant Director, to manage on a national scale investigations involving sabotage, espionage, Selective Service violations, foreign funds and travel, agents of foreign principals, sedition and related matters.

22

MR. HOOVER
DIRECTOR

MR. HARBO
ASSISTANT DIRECTOR

MR. BOARDMAN
ASSISTANT TO THE
DIRECTOR

MR. TOLSON
ASSOCIATE DIRECTOR

MR. NICHOLS
ASSISTANT TO THE
DIRECTOR

MR. ROSEN
ASSISTANT DIRECTOR

MR. BELMONT
ASSISTANT DIRECTOR

MR. TAMM
ASSISTANT DIRECTOR

MR. MOHR
ASSISTANT DIRECTOR

MR. PARSONS
ASSISTANT DIRECTOR

J. EDGAR HOOVER AND HIS STAFF

Every effort was made to avoid hysteria and possible injustices which might develop following the operation of vigilante organizations and unauthorized groups of individuals, even though their activities were motivated by the highest patriotism. All citizens were urged to report any information to the nearest FBI office without attempting to investigate or evaluate it. The response was most gratifying.

Irresponsible witch-hunting was ended. Local law enforcement officers responded enthusiastically to the Chief Executive's request to transmit data direct to the FBI office covering the territory. The information was then properly indexed, recorded and coordinated on a national basis. Representatives of the FBI visited countries already at war and gathered firsthand information on the problems beleaguering law enforcement. Then on-the-scene studies in Europe were translated into a formula for American police action in the event the United States became embroiled in a "shooting war," and by means of schools for chiefs of police and top officials, our observations were made known to the rank and file of American law enforcement. Through the FBI Peace Officers Mobilization Plan for National Defense, local officers were alerted to their wartime duties and the machinery was set in motion whereby a selected corps of police officials, already trained and experienced in certain phases of general intelligence and national defense investigations, was available to assist and supplement the work of the FBI.

This challenge by law enforcement to the nation's enemies was paralleled by the close and cordial cooperation between the officials of the FBI and the officers of the Military and Naval Intelligence Divisions. Each week conferences were held at Washington, attended by the Directors of the Military Intelligence Service, Office of Naval Intelligence, and the Federal Bureau of Investigation. Similar conferences held regularly in our Field Offices with local representatives of ONI and MIS were supplemented by daily informal conferences and communications among the three organizations.

The enforcement of peacetime statutes by the FBI continued, but our security work increased daily in tremendous proportions. Accountants skilled in bank and Court of Claims cases were used to investigate war frauds and to monitor accounts of foreign funds. Spies needed money to be successful and tried to get it by manipulating funds through a maze of dummy accounts. The FBI Laboratory expanded its already extensive facilities. From a small number of cases handled annually the total leaped into the tens of thousands.

At 1:25 P.M., Sunday, December 7, 1941, the Honolulu Office of the FBI called headquarters at Washington, D.C. It was 7:55 A.M. in Hawaii. Jap bombers were blasting Pearl Harbor! The first call sparked into action the nationwide war plans of the FBI.

The shock of the Japanese sneak attack on Pearl Harbor was registered immediately in South American countries. It made them suddenly alert to the prospects of similar attack.

For more than two years the FBI had found that enemy spying in the United States tied in closely with Axis activities among sister republics to the south. Advised of the information revealed by FBI investigations in the United States, South American countries enthusiastically agreed to co-operate. Many republics asked for FBI liaison agents to work with their own police and intelligence forces. Others sent intelligence officers to train at FBI schools.

The FBI and the law enforcement agencies of the South American countries exchanged information on all matters of mutual interest. In this way an effective Pan-American intelligence force was successfully created to oppose the destructive fifth-column activities of the Axis spy and sabotage rings in South America.

Altogether, during the period July 1, 1940, through June 30, 1946, more than 15,000 Axis operators and sympathizers in South America were expelled, interned, or removed far inland where they were harmless. More than 460 spies, saboteurs, and propaganda agents were apprehended and neutralized. Thirty secret short-wave radio stations used principally to transmit information about the United States to Germany were eliminated.

During World War II the United States did not suffer from a single act of enemy-directed sabotage, and enemy espionage activities within the United States were kept under firm control. Even in those hectic war years, the FBI became more and more concerned about a new and possibly more deadly menace to our internal security — the infiltration of Communism into practically every field of endeavor in the United States. We know that the Communists were engaged in espionage activities; that Soviet missions in the United States were staffed far beyond their needs; and that these Communist agents had perfect freedom to come and go as they pleased. At that time, however, Russia was our ally and the national climate was different from that of today. Only within the past few years has there been a real public awakening to the menace of Communism.

The work of the FBI was increased manifold by a growing awareness of this menace. Recognizing the necessity of staffing our atomic installations with loyal Americans, Congress passed the Atomic Energy Act of 1946, which placed the responsibility upon the FBI to investigate those persons who would have access to restricted atomic energy information. Under this Act, the FBI's responsibility is limited to applicant-type investigations and investigations of criminal violations of the Act. The FBI has no responsibility for security within atomic installations. The infamous theft of our atomic secrets by the British scientist, Klaus Fuchs, occurred prior to the time the FBI had any responsibility for atomic security. It was through the efforts of the FBI, working with British security authorities, that Fuchs was identified. The subsequent identification of Fuchs's associates in this country, their arrest and conviction resulted from the work of our Special Agents.

In 1952, Congress relieved the FBI of the responsibility of conducting certain applicant-type investigations, including the less sensitive jobs in the atomic energy program.

The Federal Employee Loyalty Program instituted in 1947 by Executive Order 9835 added additional burdens to the work of the FBI. Under this program the FBI was required to check the names as well as the fingerprints of Federal employees and applicants through its files. In addition, the FBI was required to make full field investigations upon receipt of information or complaints coming within the purview of the Loyalty Program.

From the beginning of the program in 1947 to May 28, 1953, a total of 4,716,390 persons were processed and their loyalty forms were returned to the Civil Service Commission with the notation, "No disloyal information." A total of 26,556 full field investigations were made by the FBI and the results submitted to the Civil Service Commission. In handling the Loyalty Program, as in our other investigations, the FBI does not make evaluations, recommendations, or express opinions. Responsibility for such action rests on the employing agencies and the Civil Service Commission.

The Civil Service Commission advised that a total of 557 persons were found unfit for Federal service, and that 6,382 had resigned prior to the completion of the investigation or the adjudication of their cases.

The new Federal Employee Security Program instituted by Executive Order 10450, effective May 28, 1953, expanded the old Loyalty Program to include other security items, such as drug addiction, immorality, alcoholism, and other factors bearing upon one's fitness to serve the Federal Government from the standpoint of security.

In the meantime, the conviction of 11 top officials of the Communist party, USA, on October 14, 1949, for violation of the Smith Act, which prohibits the teaching and advocacy of the overthrow of the United States Government by force and violence, laid the way for a broad offensive against the Communist party. Since the return of indictments in the original Smith Act case in 1948 a total of 117 persons have been arrested on such charges up to August 15, 1954, while 81 have been convicted. Prosecution is pending in numerous other cases.

The Korean aggression in 1950 brought on even more work for the FBI. On July 24, 1950, President Truman restated the Presidential Directives originally issued in 1939 and 1943 designating the FBI as the agency to investigate espionage, sabotage, and subversive activities and again called upon patriotic Americans to report to the FBI information pertaining to these matters.

The enactment of the Internal Security Act of 1950 on September 23, 1950, placed additional responsibilities on the FBI in connection with the regulation and the prosecution of the Communist party, front groups and individual party members.

On November 22, 1950, the Attorney General filed before the Subversive Activities Control Board a petition for an order of the Board to require the Communist party, USA, to register as a "Communist — action" organization as defined in the Internal Security Act of 1950. On April 22, 1953, the Attorney General filed before the Board petitions requesting orders that various organizations register as "Communist front organizations." These proceedings will require the development of evidence and witnesses necessary to establish the character of each such organization.

While FBI investigative responsibilities relating to the internal security of the country have continued to increase rather than decrease since the cessation of hostilities, its responsibilities in connection with violations of the general criminal statutes have also

27

been enlarged as, for example, by the new Federal law which prohibits the interstate transportation of gambling devices. Despite the fact that a large part of its attention was necessarily devoted to the domestic intelligence field, the percentage of convictions in FBI cases brought to trial during the 1954 fiscal year was 95.8 per cent.

These convictions, totaling 10,511, resulted in sentences totaling 27,301 years, 5 months, and 10 days. In addition there were three death sentences and five life terms. During the same twelve-month period, 14,127 fugitives were located in FBI cases and 14,492 stolen motor vehicles were located and recovered. Fines, savings, and recoveries in matters investigated by the FBI during the 1954 fiscal year totaled $60,340,749. Renegotiation Act claims investigated by the FBI and adjusted in favor of the government totaled $21,942,381.

The FBI, which is responsible to the Attorney General, continues as a service agency and carries out the directives and policies of higher authorities. Over the years the Bureau has sought to avoid injecting itself into matters of solely a local nature and adheres to this policy daily except when directed by the Attorney General or the Department of Justice to carry on specific investigative activity. For example, the FBI investigates alleged violations of the several Civil Rights Statutes upon the specific direction of the Criminal Division of The Department of Justice. It is the custom of the Bureau to advise the head or appropriate official of the agency or institution involved that an investigation is being conducted. In the 13-year period before 1939, a total of 194 lynchings occurred in the United States while in the 14 years since 1939, a total of 39 lynchings occurred. This definitely indicates a growing regard for Civil Rights throughout the United States.

Chapter I

How a Special
Agent Is Trained

THE Special Agents of the Federal Bureau of Investigation, like the criminals they hunt, are marked men. They are marked, first, because they are law enforcement officers, a calling that tends to set its followers off from their fellow men; but they are even more distinctly set apart by the training they received and the responsibilities they accepted when they became Federal Agents. Not that G-Men are turned out by crank and are alike as BB shot. Far from it. Indeed, the Bureau shies from employing a standard model candidate for reasons that are obvious: if Agents were turned out by assembly-line methods, each would be instantly recognizable. But when any employer insists on getting the best personnel available and further limits the field by applying strict qualification requirements, he is likely to find that his help falls into a definite type. So it is with the FBI.

To that extent, therefore, all FBI men tend to be alike. Today they must be college graduates; they are either lawyers, accountants, experts in languages or scientists. They are all in good physical condition; the FBI sees to that. They are excellent marksmen, especially handy with the .38-caliber revolver. Their reasoning, analytical and deductive faculties have been highly developed by intensive training methods. They run to nattiness in dress, directness in speech and aggressiveness in action.

How did they get that way? By what process did several thousand young men, drawn, as the newspapers say, from all walks of life, attain the selfless state that is the ideal of the FBI? How is it that slow, easygoing boys from Kentucky, lanky Texans and brusque New Yorkers still retain their superficial characteristics and yet think and act as one when an emergency arises? The answer lies in selection and training, plus a vigorous weeding out of those who passed preliminary tests.

Precious few misfits get past even the first barrier. In fact, few applicants get into the FBI at all. Of thousands of candidates yearly, only a few are finally selected, the number being determined by the needs of the service. The successful applicant must have a lot on the ball—the necessary educational background, excellent health, an unblemished private life and real interest in a career of Government service.

The candidate who would be a G-Man must be between the ages of 25 and 40, a graduate of a resident law school, or an accounting school graduate with at least three years' experience in commercial accounting or auditing. He must be a United States citizen, willing to serve in any part of the world. He must be at least five feet seven inches tall, but his chances will not be improved if he is unusually large. He must be capable of vigorous physical activities, but should not be an obvious strongman type. A Special Agent must not be conspicuous in appearance. He must have corrected vision of 20/20 in each eye, and he should be able to hear ordinary conversation at a distance of fifteen feet with either ear.

These are basic requirements. If an applicant lacks any one of them, he will go no further. If he has them all, he still has a hard pull ahead before he receives his appointment. He is interviewed by an Inspector or by the Special Agent in Charge at the Field Office nearest his home. At this interview the examiner tells the applicant something about the work of the FBI—that it is hard and continuous, not always exciting. Only a small portion of the work is concerned with tracking down and apprehending dangerous criminals at the point of a gun, he points out. Agents, the applicant is told, are far more likely to spend most of their time checking bankrupt accounts, interviewing witnesses, collecting evidence to be sent to the Laboratory, or writing long reports on a never-ending series of dull subjects. The prospective FBI man is told, too, of the requirements, the dangers, the confidential nature of the work; he learns that if he is accepted he will undoubtedly work long hours, that he will certainly be away from his home and family for long periods, and that he will be expected to serve on a career basis in which merit is the only basis for advancement and promotion.

If this has not daunted and dismayed the applicant too much, the interview proceeds. He is asked why he wants to join the FBI, and much depends on his answer. In a written examination to test his analytical and investigative abilities, he is asked to apply a statute to a given set of circumstances. Sometimes a practical test is added to gauge his ingenuity and initiative. The candidate may find the Special Agent in Charge extremely busy when he arrives at the Field Office for his interview, and he is told something like the following:

"There's a fellow by the name of Johnson registered over at the White Hotel. His name was given as a reference by Timothy Jones, another applicant for appointment as Special Agent. See what he knows about him."

The applicant, somewhat taken aback, would go to the hotel, where a Special Agent from the office would be planted to receive him. The candidate's approach, handling of the interview and general conduct would then be under expert scrutiny. On his return to the office the Special Agent in Charge would greet him with:

"All right, here's a stenographer. Dictate a description of Johnson and relate exactly what he told you."

One applicant, sent on such an errand, spotted a man hiding behind a newspaper in a far corner of the hotel lobby. Suspicious of the whole matter, he guessed rightly that this was his man. He interviewed the man, who said he was working for a certain automobile concern in the city. Losing no time, the neophyte telephoned to find that the auto company had no such employee on its pay roll. Back in the Field Office with his report, this applicant naturally made a good impression. He is now, incidentally, a supervisor in the Washington headquarters of the FBI.

The applicant's interview with the Inspector or Special Agent in Charge is all-important. He may not know it at the moment, but he is getting a thorough going over by a man trained in observing the character of his fellow men. While the interview is in progress the examiner notes the candidate's personal appearance and approach. Is his dress neat, flashy or untidy? (It doesn't matter if his suit is shiny or nearly threadbare, as long as he is neat and tidy.) Are his features refined, ordinary or coarse? Does he suffer from any physical defects? The applicant's conduct during the interview is broken down into a series of revealing highlights—personality, poise, speech, assurance, nervousness, tact. The level of his general intelligence is observed, and the examiner notes whether he appears to be resourceful and might have latent executive ability. His goal in life, his tastes and recreations provide further clues to his desirability as a future Agent. The application form lying before the examiner reveals the candidate's state of health, his debts, the organizations and clubs he has belonged to, his residences in the past ten years, and his arrest record, if any. Taking all these factors into consideration, the examiner writes a report on the general impression the candidate produces.

The applicant who passes both the oral and written tests has cleared only the first hurdle. There are many more to come. It is at this point that he—who may someday have the responsibility of investigating the private lives of others—is himself investigated by the FBI. The Bureau does a thorough job, leafing back in his life story to the time when he was very young. Special Agents attached to the Field Office nearest his home town are assigned to this task. They complete a file on him that reflects every aspect of his life—schools, employment, the type of his associates, his moral standing, his reputation in the community, his family background and home environment. To do this, the Agents interview not only the references named by the candidate in his application, but his schoolteachers, his high school principal, his college professors, perhaps the mayor and chief of police in his town, his neighbors, his employers and fellow workers.

When that job is finished, the FBI has an accurate estimate of the man who seeks to join its ranks. Lapses of memory or distortions of fact in the candidate's application form now stand out clearly.

The men who stand up under the Bureau's microscope are then placed on the eligible list. All they have to do now is wait until they are called. The period of waiting may be short or long, depending on the Bureau's requirements, but one day the applicant receives a telegram. It is a long, exciting telegram. It is signed "Hoover." It tells him that his application has been accepted and that he has received an appointment as Special Agent of the Federal Bureau of Investigation at a starting salary of $5,500 per annum. If he still wants the job, he is told, he must proceed to Washington at his own expense to enter the FBI Academy for training.

The successful candidate is overjoyed; he believes that his troubles are over. He is mistaken; they are just beginning.

On his arrival at FBI headquarters in Washington, the new Agent is issued manuals of instruction, a brief case, a .38-caliber revolver and his credential card. Enclosed in a black leather wallet, this card bears his photograph and informs him that he is "charged with the duty of investigating violations of the laws of the United States, collecting evidence in cases in which the United States is or may be a party in interest, and performing other duties imposed upon him by law." Woe betide the unfortunate new Agent who loses or misplaces his credentials!

After a day to settle down in his new surroundings, the Agent hears the bad news. He is strictly on probation while taking the training course of sixteen weeks. The passing grade is 85, and if he fails to make the grade, he's out. Only a few new Agents flunk the course. With this information as a bracer, the routine of the training school now hits the successful candidate full force. Classes are held from 9 A.M. to 6 P.M. with plenty of homework. (During the war new Agents went to school from 9 to 9.) After that his time is his own except that he must transcribe his notes on the day's work and get his studying done for next day. In both its mental and physical aspects, the training course is rugged. It is meant to be. It is designed to separate the sheep from the goats, the men from the boys. The training curriculum includes accounting, business, education, psychology, public speaking; social, physical, general and biological science; economics, government, personnel procedures, office management, advanced composition and practical experience. It is changed constantly to meet the changing needs of the Bureau. During the war, for example, attention was directed to such matters as sabotage, espionage and counterespionage; since the war's end, bank robberies, again on the increase, have been studied more intensively.

As we have already seen, the FBI has jurisdiction over a wide range of statutes. For that reason it is necessary that each Agent be trained and equipped to conduct an investigation involving any of the matters in which the Bureau may be involved. There would be little point in having Agents who specialized only in automobile thefts, or kidnapings, or bankruptcies. Hence the diversity of the training course and the amount of knowledge the trainee must digest are enough to daunt the ablest among them. The trainee in the

35

coming sixteen weeks will divide his time between the classroom and gymnasium in the Washington headquarters and the classrooms, ranges and practical work at the FBI Academy at Quantico, Virginia.

The student-agent will not be long in the classroom before the peculiar nature of FBI training is brought home to him. The instructor will read a statement to the class. It may be fairly long, perhaps somewhat involved.

"Now write down, word for word, exactly what I have said," he orders.

A trainee glances absent-mindedly at his watch in the course of a lecture.

"Mr. So-and-so," says the instructor, "I noticed you looking at your watch a few minutes ago. What time was it?"

In the recess period one of the new Agents spends some time looking out of the window. The class resumes.

"Mr. Smith," says the instructor, "you were looking out of the window during recess. No doubt something caught your attention. Will you describe to the class precisely what you saw?"

In many cases the trainee saw precisely nothing. Similarly, during a lecture a crash is heard from the next room. The instructor proceeds imperturbably. In a few moments comes another crash, this time louder and accompanied by confused shouts. Later a man bursts into the classroom, looks around him and runs out. When the class comes to the inevitable narration of these planted incidents, discrepancies in the accounts are almost incredible. The time between the crashes will be estimated variously at half a minute to anything up to a quarter-hour; the description of the intruder may vary from mere inexactitude to the ludicrous. But in a very short time the men learn to observe, really to see and hear things, and to describe with precision what they saw and heard.

The classroom grind is enlivened by daily sessions in the gymnasium. Every student must spend an hour a day at physical training. He learns the principles of disarming and jujitsu, not with the idea of putting them into practice, but to understand what can be done by a skilled and desperate adversary unless the Agent is constantly on guard and knows what to expect when he is taking criminals into custody or transporting them. In the gym he learns to keep his weapons out of reach of persons being apprehended, and he is taught how easy it is for a trained man to disarm an individual before he can squeeze the trigger.

From the classrooms and laboratories of the Bureau the trainees go to the FBI training facilities, located on the U. S. Marine Corps Reservation at Quantico, thirty-eight miles from the capital. Here they undergo some of the most important phases of their training— the use of firearms and practical investigative procedure. Marksmanship is so important to the FBI that men who are unable to qualify in the practical pistol course cannot be accepted for service as Special Agents, and their appointments are recalled by the Director on the recommendation of the Training and Inspection Division. When it is remembered that much of the G-Men's reputation was built on their willingness to engage desperate criminals in gun battles, the reason for this step is apparent. Skill with the revolver is paramount and every Special Agent must requalify at frequent intervals.

New Agents spend hours of "dry firing" in the gymnasium under the direction of instructors who teach them the art of holding, aiming and squeezing before they venture out to the magnificent pistol and rifle ranges the Bureau has constructed not far from the Academy. Here again the FBI tests its new men in a calculated effort to weed out the unfit. Elsewhere shooting is usually taught with the .22 rifle, fired from the prone position and using the rifle sling. There are several reasons for this: the ammunition is cheap, there is negligible muzzle blast from the weapon to scare the beginner, and recoil is nonexistent. The FBI does not use such methods. Their Agents start with the .38 police revolver, the .38 superautomatic pistol, the .30-caliber rifle, the .45-caliber submachine gun, the 12-gauge shotgun with the heaviest buckshot load, the 37-millimeter gun used for firing tear-gas shells and parachute flares, and lastly the fearsome Magnum .357-caliber revolver, the most powerful handgun manufactured in this country and a terrifying weapon to put into the hands of beginners. But that is the way the FBI does things. If there should be a few trainees in the group who can't take it, they will soon disappear.

G-Men use their guns only in self-defense, but when they shoot, they shoot to kill. It is a curious fact that men who have never before had a gun in their hands often make better marksmen than those who are familiar with firearms. One reason is that they have no bad habits to unlearn. Some of the trainees sail through the firearms course; others find it the hardest part of the curriculum and spend hours in solitary practice. Discipline on the FBI ranges is, as might be expected, rigorous and admirable. "Accidents do not happen, they are caused" is one of the FBI maxims. The new Agents have safety rules drilled into their heads so thoroughly that there are simply no accidents.

The practical pistol course is designed to teach new Agents to send their bullets into the vital parts of adversaries. The target used is a life-sized silhouette of a man reaching for his gun, and the value of each shot is determined by the position of the bullet hole. If the point of impact is located in such a position on the body as would normally result in death, the value of the shot is 2 points. Thus the 50 shots in the course, if perfectly fired, will produce a score of 100. To shoot this possible score of 100 on the practical pistol course is no mean feat. The Bureau rates it so highly that it presents a gold medal to every Agent who accomplishes it.

The course consists of 10 shots fired from the hip at a distance of 7 yards. The Agent starts with a loaded and holstered gun, starts firing at the command "Draw," reloads after his first 5 rounds, and must get all his shots off in 25 seconds. He has now only 5 minutes and 45 seconds left to fire another 40 rounds. First he retires to the 60-yard line, where he fires 5 shots from the prone position. Then he advances to the 50-yard line, where he gets away 5 rounds in the sitting position, reloads, and fires another 5 lying prone. Next he springs up to take his position at a barricade behind which he shields his body, and fires 5 shots with his left hand, followed by 5 shots with the right. In this position he allows only one side of his face and his gun hand to be visible to his opponent. The last 15 shots are fired from the 25-yard line, the first 5 from the sitting position and the remaining ten from right and left hands behind another barricade. The Agent who qualifies in this pistol course is far better trained and more highly skilled in the use of firearms than the vast majority of badmen can ever hope to be.

An electronic range is designed to speed up Agents' reactions in emergencies. Electrically operated pop-up targets bear life-size photographic reproductions of notorious gangsters—happily dead. These cutouts spring up suddenly to confront the shooter. Some of the criminals have their hands up, some are reaching for their guns, and others are armed and ready to shoot. When the targets appear, the Agent must shoot first at the one bearing the likeness of the armed criminal; he must not shoot at the unarmed man who is sur-

38

rendering. These, and other electrically operated targets utilized to train agents to hit moving objects, have electronic controls which measure the time interval between the moment the target springs into position and the instant the Agent's bullet strikes it.

Although the greater part of the Agent's firearms training is concentrated on the .38-caliber revolver, because it is the personal weapon with which he must live and on which his life may depend, his acquaintance with other arms is no less thorough. He is taught to control the bursts from the Thompson submachine gun and limit them to two or three rounds instead of pouring bullets out like water through a hose. He learns to handle the squat 37-millimeter gun that kicks like a steer, and to lob tear-gas shells accurately into a designated area. Not only must he learn to shoot, he must learn to strip down these arms, clean them and reassemble them. Understanding his weapons and knowing how they work make him a better marksman. A jammed tommy-gun in the hands of a gangster has often cost him his life, but a G-Man learns why the submachine gun is inclined to jam, how to avoid jamming, how to clear a jam quickly if one should occur. The long hours spent on the Quantico ranges pay off when men of the FBI meet up with rats of the underworld.

It is at Quantico that the new Agents put into practice the knowledge they have acquired in the classroom. FBI instruction is pre-eminently practical. It goes on the theory that in college the trainees learned something written in a book; here they will learn to do by doing. Investigative procedure and scientific crime detection cannot be learned by reading; the new Agents must do the jobs for themselves. They are taught how to use a camera, how to bring out latent fingerprints and how to identify them, how to take plaster casts of footprints and tire treads, how to conduct surveillances, how to organize crime scene searches, how to collect and pack evidence for the FBI Laboratory so that continuity of possession is assured— in short, how to do a job that hitherto has been merely theory to them. Some of the young lawyers who come to the FBI Academy have only the slightest idea of how to go about getting a search warrant or filing a complaint, for example—a highly necessary part of their work in the field.

This type of instruction is known as project training. It is intensive, ingenious and, above all, practical. It works in this manner: The class is in session, attending a lecture on automobile theft, let us say. The telephone on the instructor's desk rings. In the adjoining room another instructor, playing the part of the complainant, reports that his car has been stolen. Over a loud-speaker in the classroom the students hear his end of the conversation. They note the details given by the complainant—his name, address, where and when the car was stolen, the registration and serial numbers of the automobile, its make, color and year model. The class then holds a "skull session" on the complaint. What details are lacking? What more ought to have been elicited from the complainant? What is the next step? Questions are flying between trainees and instructor when the telephone rings again. This time it is a report of a bank holdup. A description of the robber is given, and the car used in the crime appears to tally with the description of the automobile reported stolen. Out go the trainees to the scene. They interview witnesses, bank employees, the owner of the stolen vehicle—all played by FBI instructors—and they search for clues and evidence. Back in the classroom, perhaps next day by this time, they submit their reports and thrash out their mistakes. What have they overlooked? What did they forget to do? In the midst of their arguments, which are lively and spirited, another phone call is made. This time it is a report of a hit-and-run accident—a man has been killed. What looked like a simple auto theft is building up into a complex crime of major proportions.

In the wooded lanes of the Quantico Reservation, the instructors have simulated a hit-and-run tragedy. The car is in the ditch, broken glass is scattered about, and Daisy Mae, the FBI's dummy who is "murdered" almost every hour on the hour in the interests of scientific crime detection, lies by the side of the road. The class prepares to make a crime scene search, one of the most important jobs a G-Man does. They come equipped with cameras and crime scene kits containing all the implements necessary for making plaster casts, taking fingerprints and collecting and packing the evidence. They make their pictures, take measurements, lift fingerprints, search the car, collect what pieces of evidence they can, interview witnesses and retire to prepare their reports.

At the next classroom session their reports are analyzed, evidence examined, photographs criticized, and plans of the crime scene compared. If, as is probable, the new Agents have walked all over the scene, missing angles and overlooking or even destroying evidence, they will not be spared a tongue-lashing by their instructors. And so the case goes on, link after link being forged until a suspect, again played by an FBI man, is found and apprehended. At his mock trial the new Agents appear as witnesses. They are grilled by the "defense" and once again their performance is thrashed out in class. At the end of a project of this kind, the new Agents learn the importance of picking up every scrap of information at the very beginning, for the case is so designed that one lead points the way to another. After a few such performances the groups of new Agents begin to work smoothly as a team—co-ordinated, organized, skilled—acting like men who know their business.

The new Agent receives intensive training in Constitutional Law and the Bill of Rights. He reviews the historical and philosophical basis of these documents and amendments. The importance of protecting and preserving the rights of persons under investigation is stressed again and again during his training program. The new FBI Agent learns that by virtue of his Oath of Office he has become the guarantor of these rights. He knows that any violation of such rights by a Special Agent will result in speedy and drastic disciplinary action.

At the conclusion of his training he is assigned to a Field Office. Every Special Agent is given three choices of the offices to which he would like to be sent. The assignment, however, is dependent on the good of the service and the type of experience that would be beneficial to him. It is a standing joke in the service that if a man asks to be sent to New York he will wind up in San Francisco. Matters are not arranged so simply, however. Here is a new Agent, for example. He comes from Texas and would like to be assigned to the Field Office near his home town. The Bureau looks him over: he'll make a good Agent, but he's a country boy. He needs broadening, some experience in big cities. So he draws the New York or Chicago assignment. Like all Agents, he packs his bag and leaves uncomplainingly. But despite the necessity of assigning men to posts they would prefer to do without, many of the Special Agents are located in their Field Offices of first choice, since it is the Director's policy to put men where they would like to be.

On his arrival at his first Field Office, the new Agent's real work as an FBI man begins. The Special Agent in Charge hands him a case, or more likely several cases. Each case is assigned by the SAC to the best-qualified Agent available at the moment. Therefore, it is unlikely that the new man is going to draw a top-notch case right away. At this point he remembers what his first **FBI** interviewer told him about writing interminable reports on dull cases. But whatever the nature of the case entrusted to him, it is "his" case. He solely represents the FBI in it. He handles it from start to finish. When his investigation is completed, he submits a summary report on the case to be used by the United States Attorney as the basis for action. When the case comes to trial, he will testify as a witness.

It is not to be thought that each Agent works only on one case at a time. He has numerous cases assigned to him at once, sometimes as many as thirty or forty. Although the Bureau has found that the ideal is ten cases, the current average is just about twenty per man. Some cases, of course, can be cleaned up in a day or two; others may run for months and years. If a youngster steals a car and drives it out of town over a nearby state line, for example, he will probably be apprehended in a few days, but if a ring of auto thieves is involved, it may take the Agent many months of hard work to round them up. Some reports on his cases may run as high as **400** pages. The reports of wartime espionage cases, in which close surveillances of suspects are recorded, are tremendous. The Agent's individual responsibility, therefore, is heavy. His duties are not light and his working day knows no limits.

His progress in the FBI depends solely on his work from day to day. Sixty days after he enters his first Field Office, the SAC submits an efficiency rating on his work, a report which the Agent sees and has the opportunity of discussing with his superior. Annual efficiency reports are submitted to Washington on all employees. If the Agent turns in an especially meritorious job, the Director hears about it; if he falls down badly, the Director will hear about that too. The only way the new Agent can obtain a promotion in the Bureau is by good work. There is no seniority in age or in years of service in the FBI, but the Agent also has the satisfaction of knowing that no one will be appointed to the Bureau in a position higher than that of Special Agent. Every Special Agent in Charge, Inspector and Assistant Director got there by ability. If their ability fails them, they will be relieved of their positions and will be regraded.

Facts like these keep the Special Agent on his toes. He knows he must keep on top of his job. He must go back to Washington for two weeks' retraining at least once each twenty-four months. He must keep in trim in order to pass the strenuous annual medical examination. Seven times a year he must qualify in the use of firearms. If his medical examination shows he is overweight for a man of his years and height, he will get a confidential letter from the Director drawing his attention to this fact and warning him to be back in shape within a specified time.

Discipline in the FBI ranks is strict but fair. Administrative action is never taken against an Agent without full investigation of the circumstances or without allowing him to state his case. The Agent fully earns the salary the Government pays him, and nothing more; he is forbidden to accept rewards or gratuities directly or indirectly. The personnel of the FBI is covered under the Retirement Act—a Special Agent may retire voluntarily at 50 after twenty years of service with the consent of the Attorney General, and he must retire automatically at 70.

Despite the heavy responsibilities of the work, the long hours of unremitting routine, the limited salary opportunities and the dangers inherent in criminal investigation, applications for the post of Special Agent flow into the Department of Justice in a never-ending stream. It is just as well that some of the ablest and best-equipped of the country's youth continue to feel this way about the FBI.

How one candidate became a G-Man is related in pictures in the remainder of this chapter. He is typical of the thousands of young men who aspire to serve their fellow citizens by making the United States safe to live in, by preserving respect for the law and reverence for the sanctity of justice.

The applicant's record is checked back to his childhood. His family background and his home surroundings are probed. His public school teachers are interviewed when possible; his neighbors, friends and local police officials are questioned. The documents and photographs above show that the aspiring G-Man had good grades at school, that

44

he made the football team, that he was a champion Boy Scout and took part in the school's social activities. By such thorough investigation, the FBI establishes the candidate's formative training, gains a sound idea of the kind of man who seeks to be a Federal Agent in the Bureau.

45

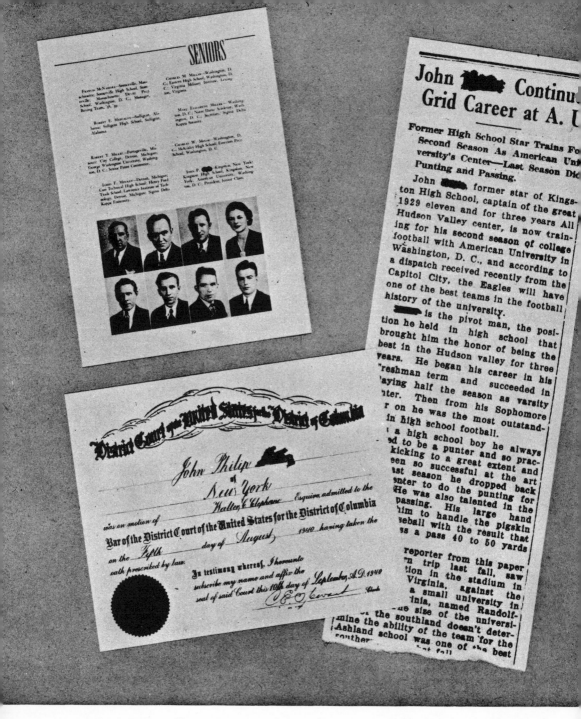

At college the candidate continued his football career, playing center for American University, and was president of his junior class. At law school, for the second semester of 1938, he scored 97 in two subjects and stood first in his class with an average of 92.12. He was admitted to the bar in the District of Columbia in August, 1940.

46

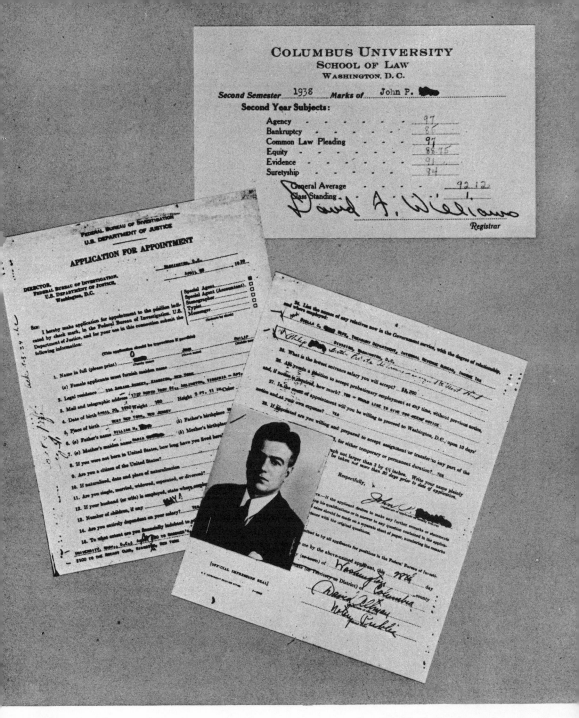

His application disclosed that he was born in the United States, of a native American father and a European-born mother. It further disclosed that the applicant was married. His health record was excellent, and the five personal references he gave were checked with the FBI with satisfactory results.

Student Agents receive a major part of their intensive training at the FBI's training facilities on the Marine Reservation at Quantico, Va. This air-conditioned building contains complete housing and mess facilities as well as elaborately equipped classrooms.

48

On their arrival at the Academy students are plunged immediately into a wide variety of subjects. Most of these are new to men who have made law or accounting their life work; one of the unusual courses they study is the recognition of facial characteristics.

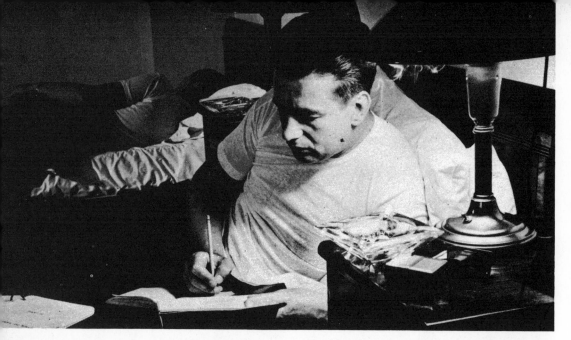

The day at Quantico is long, but not long enough for all the work that has to be done. Studies continue at night in the dormitories.

Student-Agents must familiarize themselves with the complicated apparatus of crime detection. Above is a traveling laboratory.

50

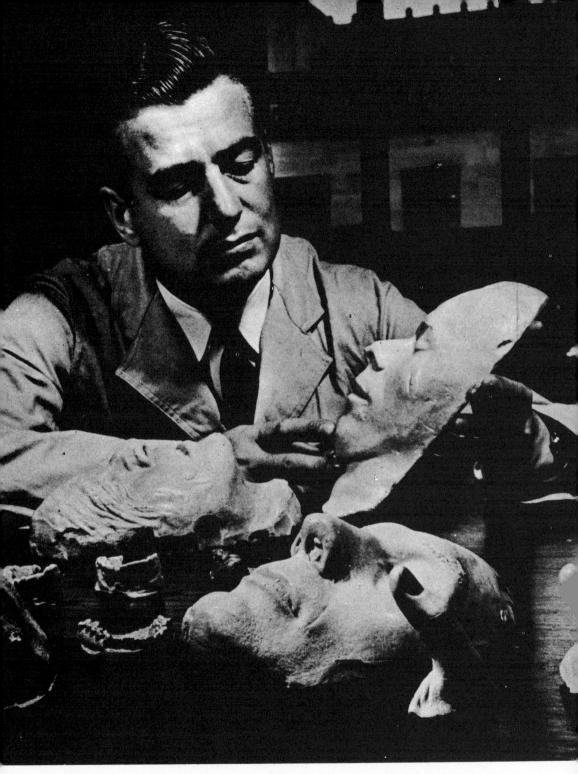

Moulage, the technique of wax modeling, is helpful in the identification of deceased persons. Here the student examines samples.

Guns are going to play a large part in the Special Agent's life, and at this point his intensive training in handling weapons begins. Here the Academy gunsmith discusses the .38 special.

FBI men bring all their gun troubles to him. He is an expert who loves handguns, and his bench in the gun vault is the daily meeting place of seekers after knowledge, for knowledge of guns is of prime importance. Students must know how to strip the various arms; clean and reassemble them. A malfunctioning gun is not of much use in an emergency, so Agents keep theirs in first-class shape.

The trainee spends hours on the ranges before he measures up to
FBI standards of marksmanship. Here, on the electronic range, he
perfects his speed shooting from the hip. Cutouts of notorious criminals spring up before him without warning, and he must select the
proper target immediately. Above, he shoots at the armed figure of
Dillinger, watches closely but does not shoot the other gangster who
is surrendering.

54

Here the machinery of the electronic range is visible. The targets are operated from a control box and many combinations are possible.

Instructor and new Agent examine the hits at close range. Note their sweat-soaked shirts as they work under the broiling sun.

It takes much practice before trainees can shoot from the hip with accuracy. In this position the sights are not lined up on the target; the shooter learns to point his gun almost by instinct.

Here four firearms instructors show what can be done with the revolver. The first man is shooting from the bridge position. The second is sighting through a mirror held between his knees. The third is firing between his legs. In all of these trick positions the gun is upside down. The instructor standing is lining up his sights by viewing the target reflection in a ring setting.

On the indoor range in the Justice Building, the new Agents perfect their tommy-gun technique by shooting tracer shells. This permits

58

them to see where their bullets are going and helps them control the submachine gun's tendency to pull upward and to the right.

New Agents learn of the high-powered radio transmitter which ties in with the Bureau's widespread communications network.

The operation of an FBI field office radio station is explained to new Agents during their training program.

60

This model city, constructed by the Exhibits Section, is complete with schools and churches, autos and traffic lights. It is used by officers attending the FBI National Academy to study traffic problems, and by Agents to learn how raids should be planned.

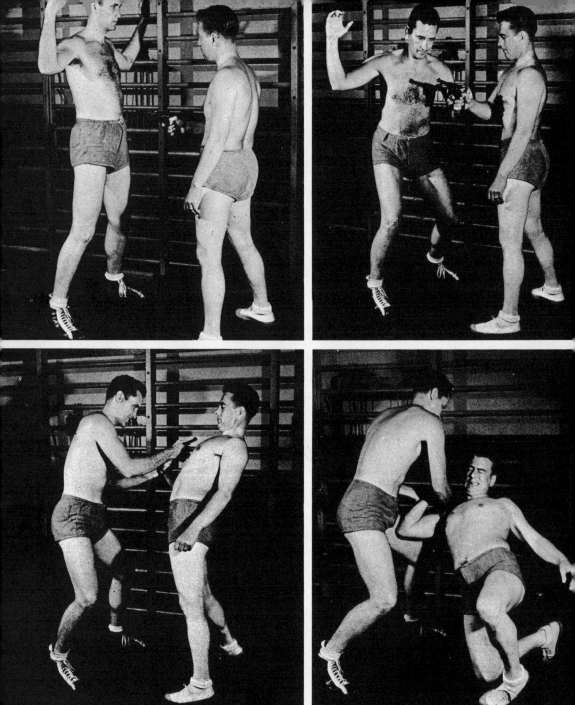

Jujitsu and disarming are among the new skills to be acquired. With a fellow student as victim, one trainee plays the role of thug and in three steps is disarmed. The students then reverse roles, practicing until they are thoroughly expert and lightning-fast.

The purpose of this training is to familiarize the men with tactics likely to be employed by criminals when apprehended. A knowledge of jujitsu comes in handy at close quarters, as can be seen from this picture of a candidate in the throes of a hammerlock.

Project training now begins. The class investigates a "crime" prepared by the instructors. Clues are carefully fashioned, witnesses are briefed and laboratory facilities are made available for research. The case opens when a Marine reports that he has discovered the "corpse" of Daisy Mae, the FBI's dummy, on the Reservation at Quantico. He leads three student G-Men to the murder scene.

64

They make a crime scene search. Other Agents take photographs, gather all clues and prepare scale drawings of the location.

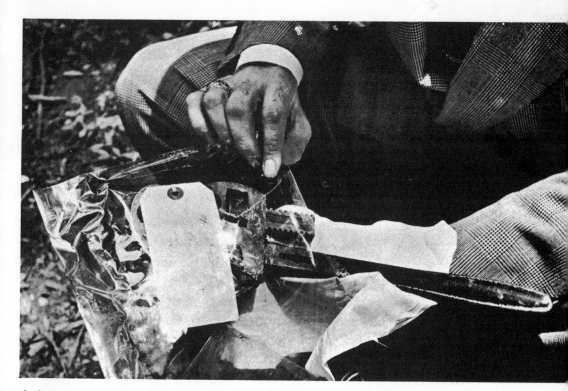

A heavy wrench is found lying near the body. It is wrapped in a cellophane envelope and tagged for identification as evidence.

Back in the classroom the trainees hold a session on what they have discovered. They have identified the woman through the contents of her purse. Fingerprints lifted from the handle of the wrench have been sent to the Identification Division. Their photographs of the crime scene are criticized. Here their theoretical training is put to the test. The instructor does not tell them what to do, nor what the next step is; he leads the discussion, points out errors and pitches into the men if they have gone badly astray. The object is to train them so that they operate smoothly as a highly organized group, each man performing his job with as little confusion and milling around as possible.

From the sergeant of the guard they learn that a gray sedan had sped through the gates.

The license number is that of a set of plates stolen in Washington the day before. The car's description is radioed to the trainees.

67

Shortly a report comes in that the car has been found abandoned in the ditch on a nearby country road. The students take serial numbers, develop latent fingerprints and search the car. Dirt scraped from mudguards is identical with that where the victim was killed. Tracing the car ownership, they find it belongs to Johnny Alpert, who has registered a nonexistent address as his residence.

An interview with the victim's father reveals that his daughter had been with a man who drove a car with a West Virginia license.

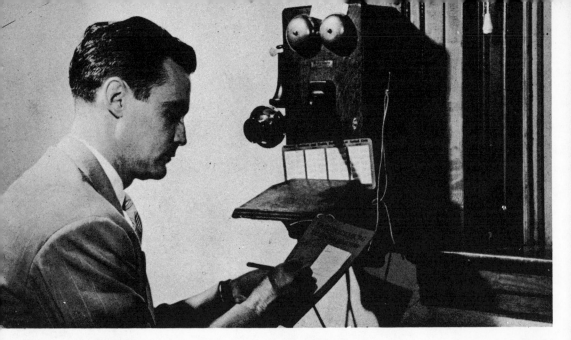

But inside the house a student Agent discovers a Washington phone number scribbled on the hall telephone book. It is that of a hotel. Alpert has checked out, but the room clerk describes him.

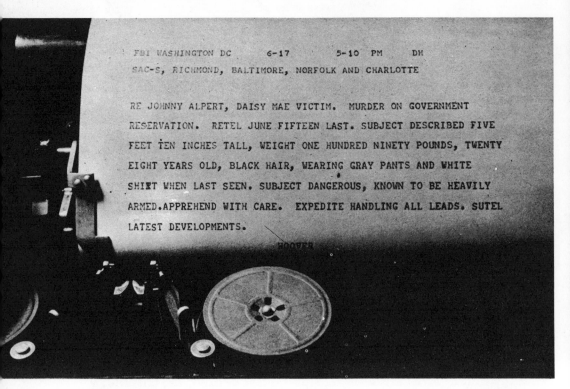

FBI WASHINGTON DC   6-17   5-10 PM   DH
SAC-S, RICHMOND, BALTIMORE, NORFOLK AND CHARLOTTE

RE JOHNNY ALPERT, DAISY MAE VICTIM. MURDER ON GOVERNMENT
RESERVATION. RETEL JUNE FIFTEEN LAST. SUBJECT DESCRIBED FIVE
FEET TEN INCHES TALL, WEIGHT ONE HUNDRED NINETY POUNDS, TWENTY
EIGHT YEARS OLD, BLACK HAIR, WEARING GRAY PANTS AND WHITE
SHIRT WHEN LAST SEEN. SUBJECT DANGEROUS, KNOWN TO BE HEAVILY
ARMED. APPREHEND WITH CARE. EXPEDITE HANDLING ALL LEADS. SUTEL
LATEST DEVELOPMENTS.

The teletype carries Alpert's description to nearby Field Offices.

From the hotel Alpert is traced to a bar he frequented; the bartender supplies further details and the Agents await his return.

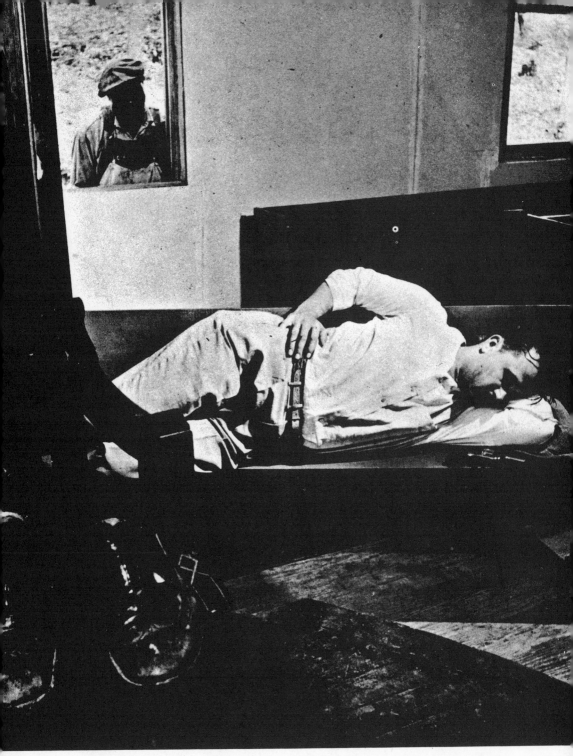

The suspect (an FBI man) turns up in a newly built church near Quantico. One of the workmen is briefed to inform the FBI about the suspicious-looking character who is in hiding there.

The new Agents examine the layout, make a scale model of church and terrain, and plan their raid on the magnetic blackboard.

They are familiar with every detail when they move into position around the church. Every exit is covered, but they take care that there are no angles of crossfire to endanger the G-Men's lives.

They order the suspect to come out with his hands up, telling him that the church is surrounded and that he has no chance of escape.

With Alpert in custody, they search him. The subject faces the wall, leaning on his hands, a position that makes a surprise move almost impossible. Note that the Agent's foot is in front of the suspect's leg. He is frisked before the handcuffs are put on.

With Alpert's arrest, his case then goes to trial. Here the same class-room technique is used. An instructor plays the part of the judge. An Agent is assigned to the accused as attorney for the defense. Other Agents take the roles of District Attorney and his aides, and the trial gets under way before the eyes of the rest of the class assembled (but not shown here) in the room at the left. Here one of the Agents in training describes the finding of the body; he identifies the photographs he took and the evidence he collected from the

76

victim's handbag. His testimony will be pounced on without mercy in cross-examination by the defense. If he slips in presenting his evidence, his instructors and fellow students will not be slow in bringing it to his attention. Every trick of a wily defense lawyer will be pulled in a mock trial such as this. By the time an FBI man gets into a real courtroom as the Government's witness, he is well schooled to stand up against bullying and hectoring methods, to be poised and to keep calm under pressure.

At the conclusion of this period of work in Washington, a high
bureau official discusses with him his first field assignment.

The new Agent meets the Special Agent in Charge at his first office of assignment.

Chapter II

How the FBI
Solves a Crime

THE detective peering through his magnifying glass, or studying the scene of a crime on hands and knees, has been a stock figure in fiction and drama since A. Conan Doyle introduced Sherlock Holmes. Holmes was on the right track, but today the investigator's magnifying glass has become a high-powered microscope.

With it he can determine, among other things, whether a bullet dug out of the victim was really fired from the suspect's gun. With his spectrograph he can take a minute speck of paint from the clothing of a hit-and-run victim and tell you what make of automobile it came from. He can determine the blood-classification group of a smoker by examining the saliva on a cigarette butt. With soil samples taken from a suspect's shoes and clothes he can tell you what locality he recently was in, and might even tell you the suspect's occupation. A lipstick stain on a lady's handkerchief will reveal its trade name and the manufacturer who made it, and a little work by an alert corps of investigators may uncover the store where it was sold and the customer who bought it. If the criminal happened to cut through wire with a pair of shears, the tool he used can be identified, for it will leave on the wire, plainly discernible to the microscope, characteristic marks that only it could have made.

The list could be extended through a hundred examples. As a man moves through his daily life, he leaves behind him a trail literally strewn with the signs of his passing. He would do well to keep on the right side of the law. If he commits a crime his chances of escaping detection are steadily narrowing. Science, in the hands of highly trained specialists, is a deadly witness against the criminal and the cold, incontrovertible evidence thus placed before courts and juries convicts the guilty and frees the innocent.

The Federal Bureau of Investigation realized early the need for scientific consideration of evidence by trained technicians. In the late 1920's, the Bureau occasionally called on an outside scientist to perform a specific examination. While the findings were usually satisfactory, the procedure was not the best, because the scientist was frequently unavailable to appear in court. In 1932, therefore, the Bureau's own Laboratory was established to make its facilities available to Special Agents in the field and to law enforcement officials throughout the country. Its technicians appear in Federal and State courts to give expert testimony without cost to local agencies. The personnel and equipment of the new FBI Laboratory have grown until today it is one of the show places of Washington.

The Department of Justice Building on Pennsylvania Avenue is much like other United States Government buildings; it is newer and perhaps handsomer than most, and it is characterized like all of them by interminable corridors. But on the seventh floor the visitor enters a new world. In place of rows of office doors are glass-paneled rooms. "No Admittance," say the signs. "This door must be kept locked at all times," read other warnings. Behind the glass panels are laboratories to which comes evidence from all parts of the country, in pillboxes and packing cases, for examination and analysis. There are laboratories where documents are examined, where blood-stains are resolved, where bullets are shot out of questioned firearms, where metals, hairs and soils are tested, where microscopic particles of matter take on new meaning and acquire significance. Apparatus ranges from the tiny utensils of microchemistry to complicated spectrographs, cumbersome X-ray machines and huge copying cameras. The FBI Laboratory has grown rapidly since its inception, but already its workers are cramped for lack of space.

The men who study incoming evidence are scientists, each a specialist in his field, each of unblemished reputation and integrity, whose character has withstood the rigorous investigation that employment in the FBI demands. Many of them are Ph.D.'s. Some hold as many as four degrees. Their job is to conduct a scientific examination of the material sent in and, as expert witnesses, to present indisputable evidence in court. Far from the scene of the crime, the Laboratory technician makes impartial and unbiased tests designed to learn the truth. He is unswayed by extraneous facts, has no personal knowledge of the principals in the crime. It makes no difference to him whether his findings are positive or negative. All he is interested in is providing evidence that can be weighed by a jury in the interests of justice.

A bullet removed from the body of a murdered man, for instance, bears plainly on its exterior surfaces a wealth of information that the expert can read with ease. The small-town sheriff who sent it in wants to know something about it; the technician can tell him a great deal. It is a .30-caliber, 180-grain bullet, he replies, and advises the sheriff to look for the 1903-model Springfield rifle that fired it. When a rifle of this model is found, the firearms expert will establish definitely whether it fired the fatal bullet. If it did, he will be prepared to go into court armed with convincing photographic proof and testify that the bullet that killed the victim came from this particular gun. The laboratory expert has merely completed another routine test. Unlike the prosecutor, he is not interested primarily in obtaining a conviction. He is interested only in seeing that truth prevails and that justice is done.

In the course of a year a tremendous amount of work is done by the FBI Laboratory. During the 1954 fiscal year, it turned out 126,518 examinations involving 112,675 pieces of evidence. Every type of test needed in the course of an investigation can be made by the Laboratory. This is done free of charge for the law enforcement agency requesting it. The list of examinations made by the Laboratory is an impressive one. Here are a few:

It will determine whether bloodstains are caused by human or animal blood. It will examine documents for invisible writing, for forgeries, erasures and handwriting identification. It will identify firearms. It will examine fragments of broken automobile headlight glass and compare them with fragments found on the headlight of the suspect hit-and-run auto. It will determine whether a tiny piece of hair is human or animal; if human, it will state whether it is head or body hair, and may indicate what racial characteristics to look for in the owner.

Here is a typical example of how the FBI Laboratory helps law officers: A police department is investigating a case in which a threatening letter has been left at a local resident's home. The police want to know who wrote it and who left it there. The Laboratory can tell much about the letter and its origin. First, the examiners can say what brand of paper was used and who manufactured it. If the letter is typewritten, the writing can be identified as that of a certain make and year of machine. If there are latent fingerprints on the letter, they can be brought out and made visible by exposing the paper to fumes of iodine crystals. With this information in hand, the local police can set about finding where the letter paper was sold, and who bought such paper in the neighborhood. They can seek the owners of all such typewriters. When the machines are located, they can obtain specimens of their writing for the Laboratory to compare with the letter. If one specimen can be identified with the extortion note, the owner's fingerprints can then be compared with those on the letter. Thus the links in the chain are welded until the guilty party is confronted with evidence that will convict him.

Here is a piece of charred, oil-soaked cloth found at the scene of a fire. Arson is suspected; this apparently was part of the material used to set the blaze. It looks like rough Turkish toweling; across it runs a broad red stripe. Beside it on the examiner's table lies another piece of evidence—a pad taken from a baby's crib in the home of a suspect. It is home-made from what looks like the same material. But there is no red striping on the pad. Are the two materials similar? If they are, it will be an important clue. It is evident that the baby pad has been washed time and again. If the material was ever striped, the dye was bleached out long ago. The fibers section establishes that the fibers are similar and the thread count identical. The baby pad is then photographed under infrared light. The results are dramatic. The infrared photograph shows a broad dark stripe running down the middle of the material! A strong piece of evidence is now in the hands of the local investigators.

Hit-and-run cases are not within FBI investigative jurisdiction but they occasionally provide the FBI Laboratory with unusual opportunities to demonstrate what it can do with tiny shreds of evidence. The hit-and-run driver does not generally consider himself a criminal, but the fear that obsesses him when he has had an accident may often cause him to act like one. He leaves the scene of the accident and thereafter often takes precautions either to have his damaged car repaired as soon as possible or to keep it off the roads for some time. Of course, many hit-and-run drivers flee because they have a criminal record, because they were driving while intoxicated or have no operator's license; but even "innocent" citizens have become panicky after an accident and departed in fright.

A careful search of the crime scene may reveal only a few pieces of glass broken out of a headlight, foglight, or parking light lens. In the FBI Laboratory, these pieces of glass are examined and may be retained for future comparison with fragments of glass from suspect cars. When the car is found, bits of glass remaining in the headlight can be compared with those found at the scene, and it is frequently possible to determine whether the two sets of fragments came from the same lens. However, if the lens cannot be reconstructed in part from the known and questioned fragments by matching the broken edges, the Laboratory examiners can determine whether they are chemically similar and have the same refractive indices. It may then be stated that the two sets of fragments could have come from the same lens.

With the suspect car located, the police can go further with their search. They can examine it minutely, looking for hair and fibers caught on protruding parts, noting damaged spots and searching them for traces of blood and material. Recent repairs and paint jobs are also noted. There is frequently enough paint on the clothing and body of a hit-and-run victim to help identify the death-dealing automobile. At this point, the Laboratory men can turn some of their neatest tricks. They can take a minute scrap of paint found on the clothing of the victim or at the crime scene and determine if it could have come from the suspect automobile. They can do it in two ways: by spectrographic analysis and under the comparison microscope.

The spectrograph (an optical instrument) makes use of the principle that each chemical element emits a unique light when burned. Thus it is possible to analyze inorganic substances although they are present in amounts so small as to be barely visible to the naked eye. The pin-point sample of paint, for example, is placed in a small crater in the end of a carbon electrode and is burned in an electric arc. The light it emits is focused through the prisms of the spectrograph and is thus broken down into its component colors. A photographic film records in black vertical lines of varying density the colors present in the flame, in the same sequence as they appear in the spectrum. Thus the technician can determine what colors were present in the flame and identify the various elements present in the specimen. From the density of the black lines he can judge the amount of each element present. If he has a sample of paint from the suspect's automobile, he can discern whether the two pieces of evidence are identical or dissimilar. If the suspect car has not yet been located, he can declare that the paint came from a certain make, year, and model of car, after reference to the National Automotive Paint File which the Laboratory maintains. This paint file contains specimens and specifications of auto paints from passenger vehicles.

The spectrograph is also used to analyze such material as particles of metal adhering to the cutting edges of tools and instruments, such as a hacksaw blade suspected of being used to cut through a brass lock, or pliers that may have cut wire. Police investigating the disappearance of 300-pound copper ingots from the plant of a brass and copper company found a pair of work gloves at the home of a suspect. Preliminary examination showed that they appeared to be impregnated with copper dust which might have come from the surface of copper ingots. Examination of the gloves in the FBI Laboratory revealed the presence of copper dust on fingers and palms, and when particles were analyzed in the spectrograph, they were found to be identical in composition with the metal in the ingots.

In addition to his spectrographic analyses of paint specimens, the Laboratory technician may also cut cross-sections, mount and examine them under the comparison microscope, a two-tube microscope so arranged that the specimens to be compared are mounted under each objective. The images thus seen converge and the technician is enabled to match similarities, such as color layers, to show that the two specimens bear identical characteristics. Automobile bodies are painted in several layers, each layer usually of a different color and thickness. Therefore, if the known specimen taken from a spot on the car near the point of impact is composed of layers of paint of the same colors and thicknesses as the questioned sample taken from the victim or some other object struck by the car, there is strong proof that the two samples come from the same automobile.

A few years ago a gang of bank robbers in the Middle West practised their profession with considerable success and for longer than usual. They were in the habit of escaping by automobile, but police officers failed to recognize their car at its appearance in another holdup. When the FBI finally broke the case, the reason became apparent. The getaway car had been painted no less than nine times! There is a microscope slide of a cross-section of that paint job on exhibition in the FBI Laboratory today. The layers of browns, blues and greens are as distinct as a picket fence.

The National Automotive Paint File is only one of the standard files kept in the Technical Laboratory for quick reference. There is an ammunition file containing the cartridges of all American manufacturers, from the short .22 to the powerful .357 Magnum. Thus when a bullet is submitted to the Laboratory for examination it can be identified as to weight and caliber by reference to the file. If the ejected shell case is also available, it can provide further evidence pointing to the gun from which it was fired, for on its base will be the distinctive, if microscopic, marks made by the firing pin, breech face and extractors.

Footprints and automobile tire tracks are frequently important clues to the solution of crime cases, but they are worthless unless preserved or reproduced for further reference. The modern technique, as we shall see in this chapter, is to make a plaster cast of the impression, which can then be measured and compared with the file of tire treads or rubber heels maintained in the Laboratory. The tire tread file contains blueprints of the specifications and measurements of some 1,750 designs of United States and foreign tire patterns, and the shoeprint file contains some 2,500 various types of rubber heel, sole and half-sole designs, trademarks, and insignia. By means of these files it is possible to identify a particular tire or shoe as the one that left an imprint at the scene of crime.

Similarly, files of wood, watermarks, hairs, and fibers, electrical wires, and the writing of practically every make of typewriter in use in the United States are available at the Laboratory for comparison with evidence sent for examination.

Some of the work carried on in the FBI Laboratory is unbelievably precise. In the document section where handwriting, papers and inks are studied, there are balances of the greatest delicacy. It is possible to weigh a piece of paper, scribble your name on it, weigh it again and determine the weight of the graphite on it. In spectrographic analyses of minute particles of matter, it has been possible in some cases to detect as little as 1/100,000 of 1 per cent of certain elements.

Evidence comes to the Laboratory in tiny packages and in huge packing cases, sometimes containing heavy machinery, metal parts and castings. During the war a considerable portion of the Laboratory's facilities was devoted to the detection of sabotage, fraud against the Government and criminally slipshod workmanship. The examiners can determine the details surrounding the breaking of a piece of metal, such as whether it gave way due to stress or overload, by studying its crystalline structure with the metallograph, a precision optical instrument that identifies crystalline characteristics. Armor plate for ships and tanks and other war equipment was tested to find out if it had been properly welded or if workmen had taken short cuts to increase their piece-work wages. In the course of these examinations, the FBI technicians discovered bridge welds and slug welds in casts that were supposed to be solid.

Another important instrument used to examine suspected metal parts is the magnaflux, which discloses the presence of cracks in ferrous objects. This equipment works on the principle that if a magnetizable part, such as an axle, is placed in a magnetic field, that field distributes itself uniformly through the metal, provided there are no fissures or discontinuities in the part which would deflect and distort the field. When the object has been placed in the magnetic field, magnetized pigment is then sprayed on it. If there are cracks in the metal this pigment orients itself around these breaks, indicating their position in a highly visual manner. For its wartime needs the Laboratory acquired a tensile tester capable of exerting a variable load up to 20,000 pounds on the material to be tested.

Blood examinations are among the most frequent type of test in the field of chemical investigation in the crime Laboratory. In murders, assaults, and other cases of violence, the suspect is likely to affirm that spots found on his clothing are paint spots, or that he was killing chickens, or that he had a nosebleed and the stains were thus caused by his own blood. It is a simple matter for the expert to determine whether the stains are indeed human or animal blood. If human blood is present, the examiner then proceeds to find out if it is the same type as the suspect's blood. If the blood on his clothing is not in the same group as the blood in his veins, the suspect is not telling the truth, and the investigation has moved forward another important step. If the bloodstains should turn out to belong to the same type as the victim's blood, powerful corroboration has been given to the weight of evidence against the suspected person. The chemical Laboratory maintains a collection of antisera for various animals — rabbits, horses, chickens, deer, etc. — against which unknown specimens are checked.

Another reservoir of information in the FBI Laboratory is the

National Fraudulent Check File, an immense collection of bad checks contributed by law enforcement agencies in every state. The file contains some 11,000 samples of the handiwork of check flashers, those glib individuals whose stock in trade consists of a stack of blank checks, a protective check-writing device, a small printing press, perhaps, and a fast line of talk. Whenever a new fraudulent check is received in the Laboratory, it is compared with this file in an attempt to determine who passed it. Over 50 per cent of the checks searched through the files are identified with checks previously examined. Sometimes it is possible to advise the officers working on a case in what region the suspect may now be found, or to report that he has already been apprehended.

Bad-check artists roam the country, trying to evade the law from state to state as they issue checks drawn on nonexistent business firms and signed with fictitious names. In one case 192 checks received in the FBI Laboratory were identified as having been written by the same person, who had used dozens of names in his career of fraud. In addition to expert scrutiny of handwriting, the Laboratory compares typewriting, check-protector impressions and printing jobs done on the bogus checks.

So thoroughly is the examiner's work done that evidence thus obtained is most convincing when he appears in court as an expert witness. Armed with photographs of the questioned material, compared with known specimens, he points to similarities or shows how they differ. Where possible, he demonstrates the point visually. He exhibits photographs of bullets under the comparison microscope, showing the suspect bullet's striations corresponding exactly with imperfections of the instruments that caused them. He produces enlarged photographs showing fibers from the suspect's clothing compared with fibers found at the crime scene, each composed of the same number of threads, of the same colors and with identical chemical characteristics in the dyes. In the witness box the technician is not called on to do much talking. He identifies the material he examined and then says in effect: "This is what I found." Thus nothing is left to the imagination of the jury. Impersonal and objective testimony of this kind has proven highly effective in the courtroom.

To show precisely the painstaking work in the field and in the Laboratory that precedes the presentation of this evidence in court, Special Agents of the FBI enacted the hypothetical case pictured on the following pages.

THE TIDINGS CASE

Jaffrey Tidings, a wealthy eccentric, disappeared from his home in New Canaan, Connecticut. Because he lived alone with the exception of a few servants, including his housekeeper, Mrs. Harper, and often made unannounced trips for a week at a time, his disappearance went unnoticed at first. After Tidings had been gone several days, however, Mrs. Harper received a note. It contained the combination of his safe and instructed her to open it, take out a steel box and leave it behind a rock on the Parkway intersection outside of New Canaan. The note was written on an envelope addressed to Tidings, and the writing was undoubtedly his. But its contents and abrupt phrasing indicated it had not been written voluntarily. Mrs. Harper guessed correctly that her employer had been kidnaped. She telephoned the local police, who notified the FBI.

The day the case was referred to the FBI, Tidings' body was found (opposite page) in a deserted summer shack in upstate New York. Two boys, out squirrel hunting, had looked through a shattered windowpane and seen the body slumped in a chair, with a pool of blood on the floor. Special Agents of the FBI went into action. How they solved the case is pictured on the following pages.

FBI Agents began collecting all possible evidence. Wallboarding where a bullet lodged was cut out and carefully packed.

Plaster-of-Paris paste poured over a tire track found near the cabin was allowed to harden, then removed for identification.

Bloodstained floorboards were cut out in thin slivers and put in a pillbox for mailing to the FBI Laboratory.

Papers were taken from Tidings' pocket to be examined later for latent fingerprints other than those of the murdered man.

The cast of a heelprint outside the cabin was marked to show the area in which it was found. The Agent initialed and dated it.

Two more clues were found. An automobile had grazed a tree, leaving a trace of paint. Threads were noted hanging from a branch.

To the FBI Laboratory came the evidence from the Tidings kidnaping: bullets, bloodstains, tire tread and heelprint casts, paint speck, threads, and the papers from the dead man's pocket.

In the Laboratory the bullet embedded in the wallboard was dug out. The examiner took great care not to mark its surfaces.

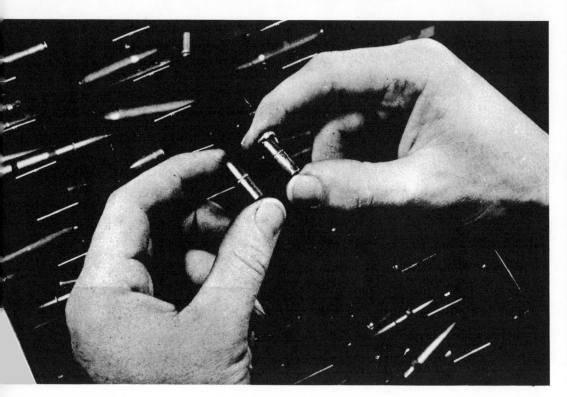

As a first step the bullet was checked through the standard ammunition file. It was found to be a .30-caliber slug.

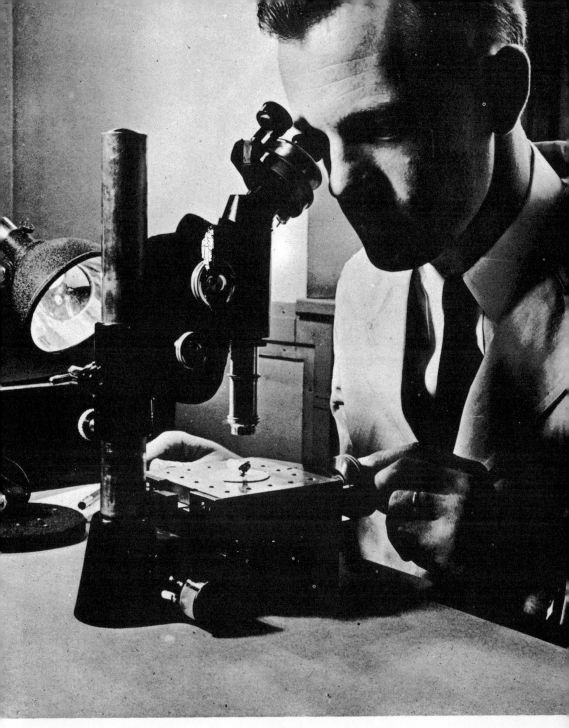

The lands and grooves carved on the bullet by its passage through the rifle were measured and compared with the rifling specifications of American arms manufacturers. They revealed that the bullet had been shot out of a Model 99 Savage, caliber .30-30.

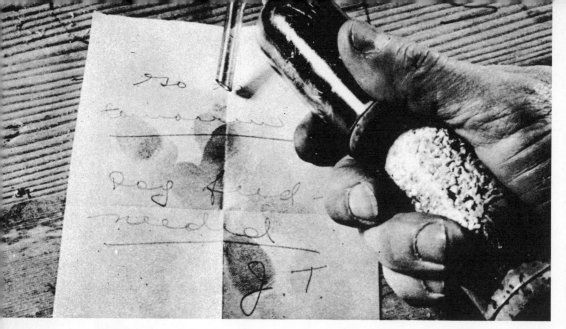

When one of the papers found in Tidings' pocket was treated with fumes from iodine crystals, fingerprints began to appear.

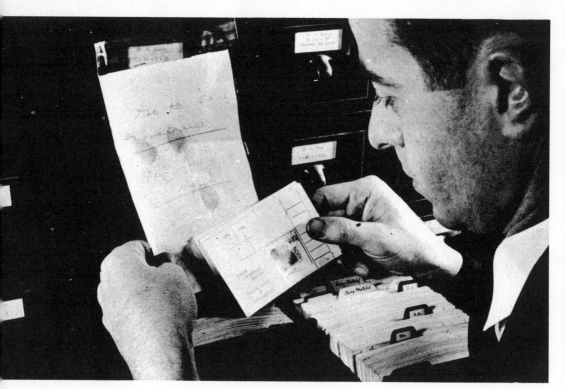

The fingerprints on the note were searched through the single-fingerprint file as one means of identifying the suspect.

Tidings' own fingerprints were located in the civil file and compared with the prints on the note. Thus his impressions were eliminated.

Meanwhile, new clues made their appearance. The two boys who found Tidings' body in the shack reported they had seen a man near the scene walking into the woods carrying a rifle. They identified him as a neighbor, Arthur Miller.

Special Agents questioned Miller immediately. In his room they found a Savage rifle of the same model and caliber as fired the suspect bullet. A pair of bloodstained socks in his closet built up the case against him, but Miller protested that he had shot a deer some time previously, and its blood had spattered his socks when he was dressing out the animal. His rifle and socks were sent to the Laboratory and Miller was put under surveillance.

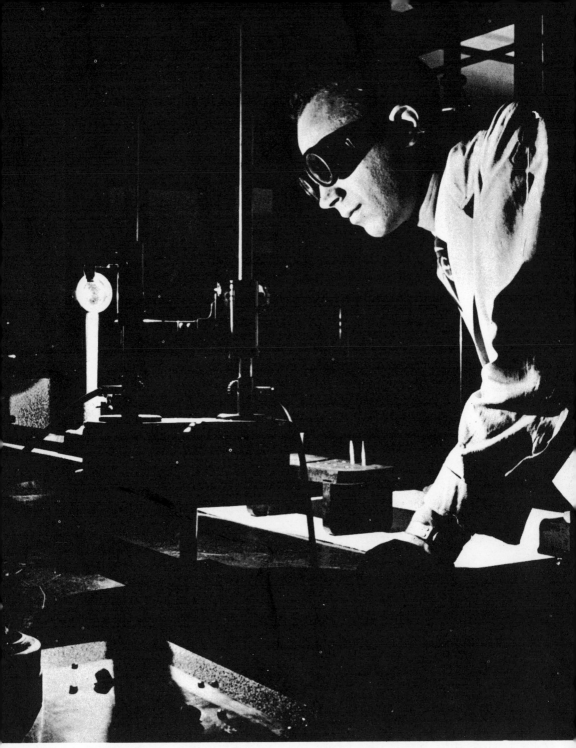

At the Laboratory, the speck of paint left by the suspect car as it grazed the tree was burned in the arc of the spectrograph to determine its chemical composition and hence its origin.

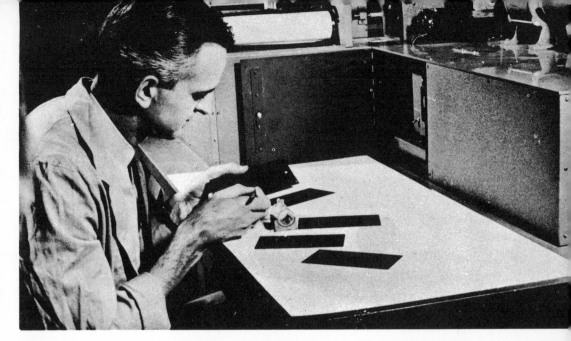

By comparing the sample with the standard paint file it was possible to determine the make, year and model of the car it came from.

An examiner compared the spectral lines of the elements in the paint specimen with a known sample, as further identification.

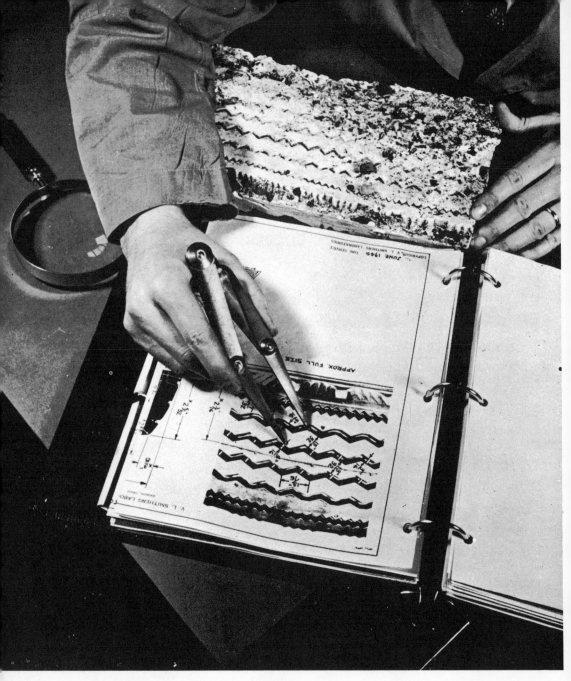

Another examiner compared the cast of the tire track with the tire tread file, measuring its dimensions with calipers and checking them against a blueprint. The shred of paint showed the car that drove through the brush was a dark green Plymouth. A report on the car was broadcast to police, who located one corresponding to the description in a parking lot. The tire tread evidence was checked satisfactorily against the tires on the car.

104

This car was searched thoroughly. A lipstick-stained handkerchief was found in the glove compartment, hair was discovered on the rear seat; a checked hunting shirt lay rolled up on the floor. This new evidence was hurried to the Laboratory in Washington.

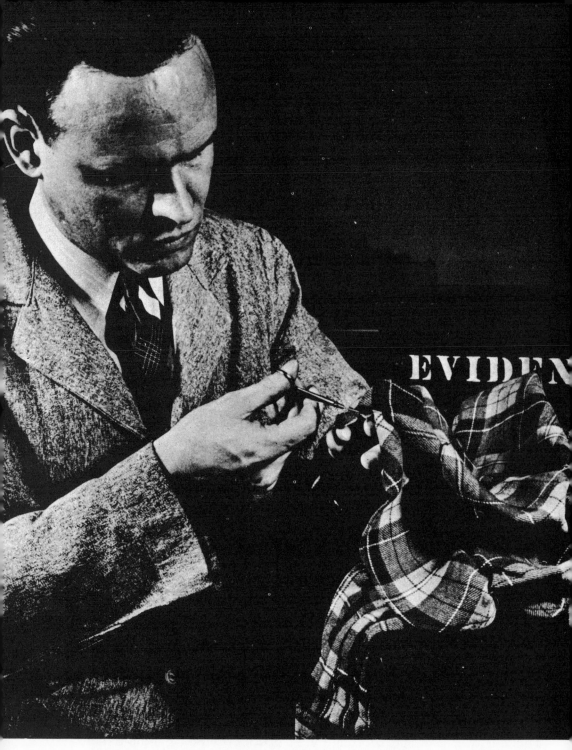

There, in the hairs and fibers section, an examiner cut off a small portion of the shirt for comparison with the torn threads found hanging from the tree at the scene of the crime.

106

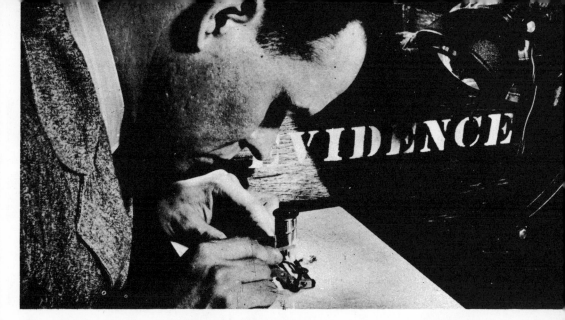

He compared the two pieces under a thread counter, noting the number of threads per inch, the type of weave, direction of twist.

Threads were then pulled out of the two specimens. Those from the threads found at the crime scene were lettered K (known) for the dye test above; those from the shirt were lettered Q (questioned). The dyes were extracted chemically, and the colors were then compared by means of a spectrophotometer.

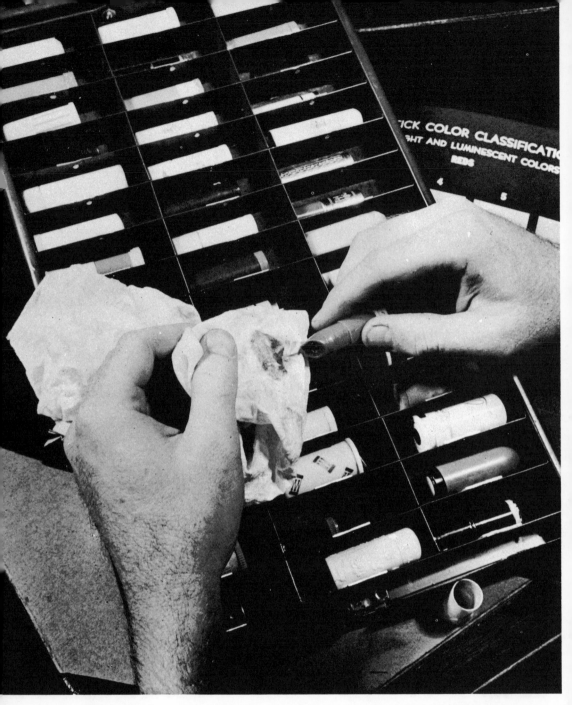

The lipstick stain on the handkerchief was analyzed by spectrograph and was then checked through the lipstick file to identify it. Through its distributors, the search for its purchaser was narrowed to a small town not far from the deserted shack. Agents began the tedious task of questioning customers of stores that sold this brand of lipstick.

108

One of those questioned was Edna Benson, a waitress in a nearby diner. She was plainly frightened when the FBI men asked her what she knew about the Tidings kidnaping, and gave evasive and contradictory answers. As the Agents left, one of them deftly plucked one of her blonde hairs from her shoulders. She was placed under close surveillance.

The hairs from Edna Benson's head and from the auto seat were embedded in wax and cross-sections were cut on the microtome.

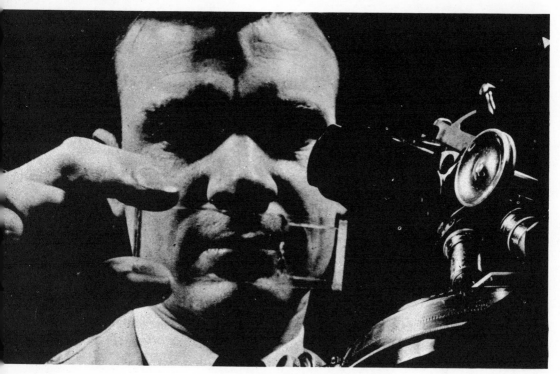

Under the research microscope, the hairs were found to be identical in size and characteristics. The hair found on the automobile seat could thus have come from Edna Benson's head.

Meanwhile, the Special Agents in the field now knew enough about the Tidings case to return Miller's gun and to tell him that he was no longer under suspicion. Here is what cleared Miller:

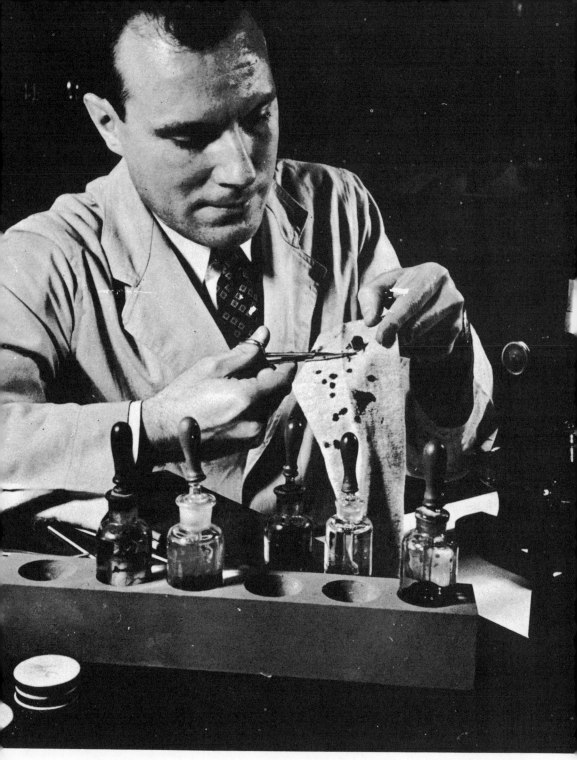

The blood spots on his socks were cut out in the Laboratory and put in a small test tube with a normal saline solution. After soaking, the test tube and its contents went into the centrifuge.

112

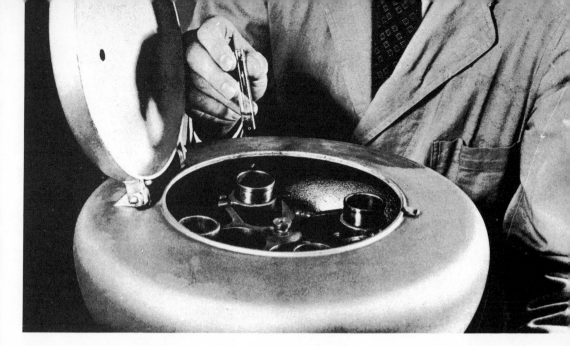

After centrifuging, the clear fluid which had risen to the top was removed by a pipette and was placed in another sterile test tube.

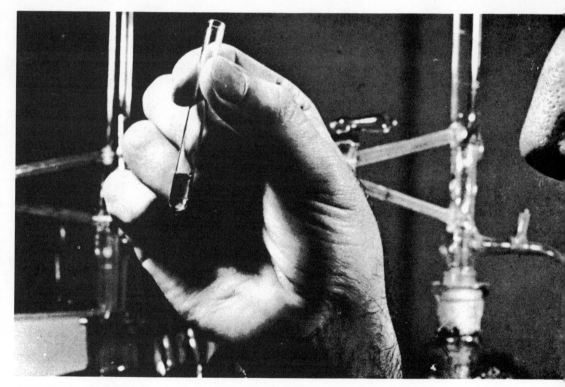

Anti-human blood serum was added. The cloudiness between the solutions showed the stains were not caused by human blood.

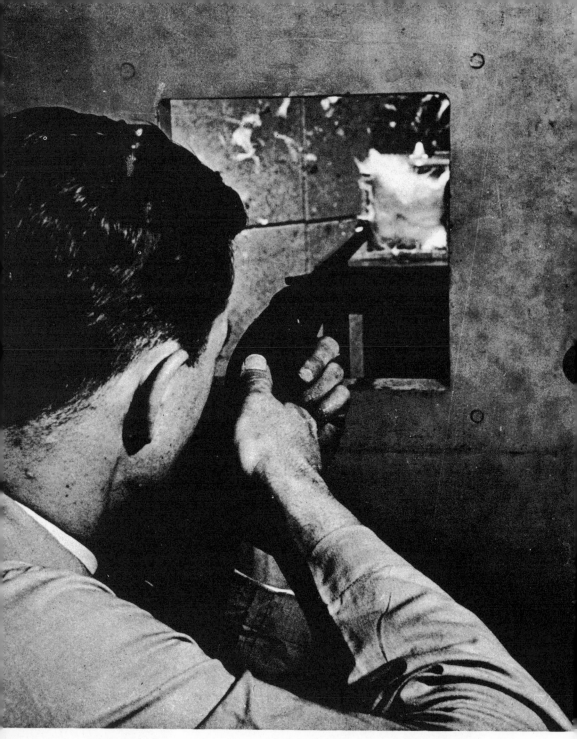

Miller's rifle was fired into the bullet-recovery chamber. The test bullet, here seen hitting the wad of cotton waste with which the box is packed, was removed from the cotton, which it had wound round itself, and then was compared with the questioned bullet.

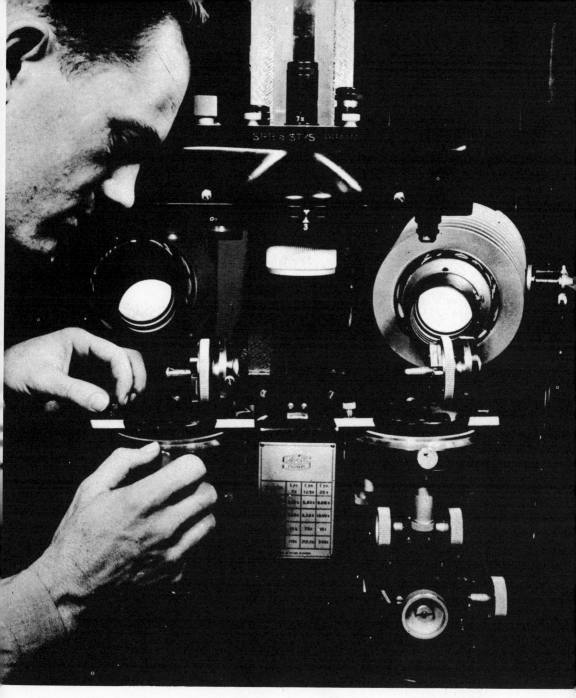

Here the test bullet (right) and the bullet found in the shack (left, with flattened point) were mounted on the twin stages of a comparison microscope. Through the single eyepiece the markings left by the rifle barrels were compared. This examination proved that the suspect bullet was not shot from Miller's rifle but from another. Thus Miller was cleared of suspicion.

115

Confronted with the evidence developed in the laboratory—that the lipstick stains on the handkerchief matched the type of lipstick she used, and that her hair was identical with strands found in the car—Edna Benson broke down and confessed her part in the kidnaping. She had accompanied her boy friend, George Foster, when he and Steve Mason held up Tidings and forced him to enter their car. She signed her name to a statement implicating the two men.

The girl then agreed to lead the FBI Agents to the hideout of Mason and Foster. "That's where they live," she told them, as she pointed out a tawdry rooming house. The Agents looked over the building and prepared to make their raid.

The FBI now acted swiftly as it closed in on the two suspects. One of them was believed to be a killer, armed and desperate, so the

Agents took precautions against a surprise move. With the house
surrounded and its exits guarded, the men were apprehended.

In the men's closet one of the Agents found a pair of shoes. They were caked with mud, and the rubber heels looked as if they might be those that left impressions at the crime scene. The shoes, the last link in the kidnaping, were sent to the Laboratory.

There it was proved by comparison and measurement that the heel-prints left at the shack were made by the shoes found in the arrested men's closet. To prove it beyond doubt, a little of the soil was scraped off the shoes.

This mud, along with a sample of the soil in the vicinity of the crime, was put through a mineral separation test. Here the heavy minerals can be seen settled at the bottom of the flasks. Further tests showed the two soils to be identical.

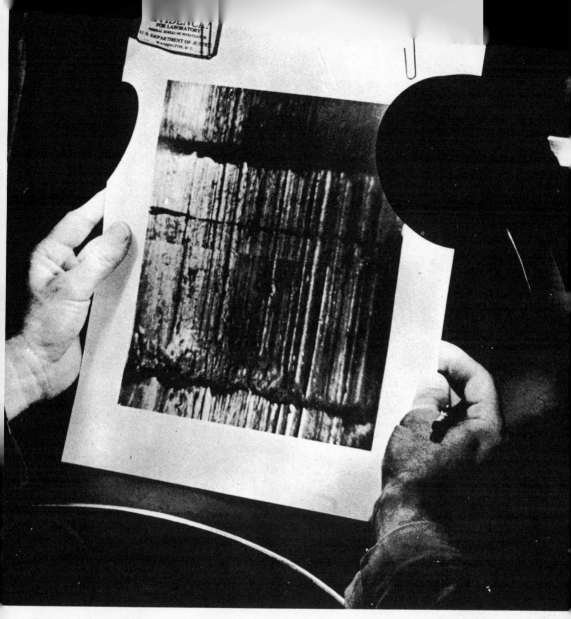

Confronted with the wealth of evidence against them, Mason and Foster confessed. Mason, standing guard outside the shack, shot Tidings when he tried to escape. Foster was with Edna Benson at the time. When he returned, they rifled the body, hid the gun nearby, abandoned the car and fled to the rooming house to hide until the case blew over. A last bit of evidence came from the Laboratory to clinch the case. A firearms expert (above) examines an enlarged microphotograph of the fatal bullet and one fired from Mason's gun. The marks on the two bullets coincide exactly, proving that Mason's gun was the murder weapon.

MALE DEAD FILE
DICKINSON
DOWN
DEAD
John Herbert Dillinger
Springfield, Ill.
Dayton, Ohio.
Crown Point, Ind
DILLI

Chapter III

Some of the

FBI's Most Famous Cases

Less than two decades ago, Americans lived in a gang era when organized bands of case-hardened criminals terrorized the country with killings, kidnapings, armed robberies and internecine warfare.

So widespread were the activities of these mobs that they threatened for a time to upset the balance of law and order. Gang lords with private armies at their disposal, well equipped with arsenals of first-class arms and fleets of speedy, bullet-proof automobiles, divided territories among themselves and stood guard over them with appalling ferocity.

Those were the days when prison breaks were commonplace; when hardened convicts left jail at will, buying their way to freedom; when gullible parole boards turned loose known killers and enemies of society to resume their preying on the public; and when political bosses shielded murderous racketeers and provided them with hideaways.

Yet, with all this, there was a tragic gulf between the nation's conception of these mobsters and what they really were. Newspaper headlines blazoned the careers of such anti-social misfits as John Dillinger, Alvin Karpis, Fred and Arthur Barker, Pretty Boy Floyd, Roger Touhy and the Brady Gang. Their names were so familiar to the American public as to become part of everyday speech. The criminal acts of these desperate men became not murders and robberies but escapades regarded with a form of admiration.

Sob sisters penned romantic pictures of these gunmen and their molls, and Hollywood, not to be outdone, portrayed them as characters who had unhappily taken a wrong step (through no fault of their own), but who would no doubt return to the straight and narrow. Adolescent hero-worship turned from the cowboy of the Wild West to the gunman of wilder Illinois, and the language of the underworld pervaded the speech of America's youth.

It was a situation that is hard to understand, even to remember, now. But it was no longer ago than 1934 that the FBI, armed with new authority—and for the first time with guns to back it up—began to clean out the gangsters and kidnapers, the shyster lawyers who defended them and got them off, the crooked doctors who dressed their wounds and tried to alter their appearances, the harborers who sheltered them, and the bill changers who provided unmarked bills for "hot money."

Only a few facts and figures are needed to recall the era when gangsters' funerals were elaborate ceremonies with bronze caskets, thousands of dollars' worth of flowers, and the sidewalks lined with onlookers. During the twenty years to 1934, an estimated 2,500 banks in the United States were robbed. The underworld was estimated to number forces greater than the number of men who enlisted in the United States Army in the first World War. In 1933 it was estimated that there were 1,300,000 serious crimes known to the police. This figure, it should be noted, was regarded as a minimum. In 75 per cent of these cases no one was brought to justice. In 1934, in 1,285 cities with a population of 49,000,000, there were 46,414 robberies, 28,117 aggravated assaults, 190,389 burglaries, 380,212 larcenies and 142,823 auto thefts.

In 1935, the nation's law enforcement officers killed nearly 400 members of the underworld who resisted arrest. Yet crime increased. There was more crime, in fact, and fewer convictions than in any other country. Fewer indicted criminals were convicted here than anywhere else. Fewer criminals were caught; it was easier to "get away with it" in the United States than in any other civilized land. More felons escaped punishment through releases on probation and more prisoners were released on parole after serving only the minimum portion of their sentences. To a great extent the same is true today, except that the public attitude is stiffening. In one year, of 85,767 prisoners released, more than half were released prior to the expiration of their terms. Almost 33,000 were paroled, and half of the prisoners showed previous arrest records.

126

At the period when gangsterism was at its peak, many of the nation's police departments were inept and incompetent because of political control. Fingerprinting was frequently regarded with amused contempt; guns were carried by men who had no idea how to use them safely and effectively.

Local law enforcement agencies resented and resisted attempts of the Federal Government to enter the field of crime repression. Thus were born the distrusts and suspicions that were removed only by the constant good will and cooperation shown to other agencies by the FBI once it had assumed the role it plays today. But others, too, had adopted this attitude. Legalists had long opposed the entrance of the Federal Government into this sphere, except where offenses had been committed against the Government. (In fact, J. Edgar Hoover has always led the fight against the creation of a national police force. He holds that the first line of defense is the home-town police, and that the responsibility should rest with them.) Interstate crime was uncontrolled, and while the existing Federal law enforcement agencies were confined to narrow limits of jurisdiction, it flourished until the country was in the grip of the gangster. The problem was to close the gap between the Federal and State jurisdictions without infringing upon the fields of State and local authorities.

That problem was solved, as we have already seen. The FBI was relieved of many of its restrictions. When its jurisdiction was extended to cover kidnaping, extortion, anti-racketeering, bank robberies, flight to avoid prosecution, and killing Federal officers, the twilight of gangsterdom was at hand. In three years of the gangster era, the FBI brought about the conviction of 11,153 persons for violations of Federal laws, including 152 bank robbers and more than 330 kidnapers and extortionists. In that era, for every dollar spent in the operation of the FBI, seven dollars were returned to the taxpayers in the form of savings, fines and recoveries. In 1935 alone, there were 40 convictions under the Federal kidnaping law, and $150,000 in ransom money was recovered. This era of gang rule has long closed. It was ended by the FBI in an unrelenting warfare that lasted until the mobsters were taken prisoner or killed.

Some of the most famous cases in the Bureau's files are picturized in this chapter. They were re-enacted in Chicago by professional actors, with the roles of G-Men portrayed by Special Agents.

THE BARKER-KARPIS GANG

One of the deadliest and longest-lived gangs in criminal annals was the Barker-Karpis outfit and its many associates. They preyed ruthlessly on law-abiding society, lived luxuriously on their booty, and left a trail of death behind them. Headed by a resolute and domineering woman, they looted and killed for more than a decade.

Kate Clark led a happy, normal childhood in the Ozarks near Ashgrove, Missouri. In 1892 she married George E. Barker. She bore him four sons—Herman, Lloyd, Arthur and Freddie. Early in her married life she began to long for money, for extravagant clothes and elegant furnishings. The family moved to Tulsa, Oklahoma— all but the eldest boy Herman, who had already departed to seek fame and fortune in the ways of crime. Ma Barker conceived the plan of training her younger sons along the same lines and living off the proceeds. Accordingly, she taught them to become cunning criminals. When they were arrested for petty infractions of the law she would persuade the police to release them in her custody and then upbraid the boys for being so stupid as to get caught. Her reputation began to spread in the underworld; her sons' gangster friends began to frequent their home, and to them Mrs. Barker was known as "Ma."

Arthur R. Barker   *Kate Barker*

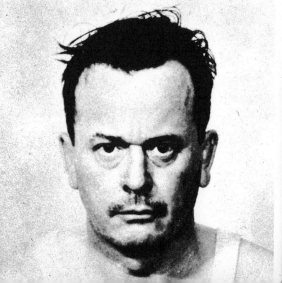

By the 1920's, the boys had run the gamut of crime from larceny to murder, and Ma had prospered on the earnings of her deadly brood. By the end of the decade, their careers had come to a temporary halt. Herman had committed suicide rather than submit to arrest for murder. Arthur (Doc) was serving a life term in Oklahoma State Prison, guilty of murdering a night watchman. Lloyd was in Leavenworth for 25 years for robbing the U.S. mails; Freddie was in Kansas State Penitentiary for burglary and larceny. Yet two of them were to be released to continue their careers of stealing and murdering! At this point Ma discarded George Barker and bestowed her affections on one Arthur Dunlop, a younger man and much handier with a gun.

Before negotiating his release from jail, Fred Barker became acquainted with Alvin Karpis, who already had an impressive career in crime. When Karpis regained his freedom, it was only natural that he should join the Barker gang. By 1931 Fred and Karpis had shot a sheriff while holding up a store in Missouri. The gang fled to St. Paul, and its members lay low until their landlady's son recognized photographs of Fred and Karpis in a detective magazine. He notified the police, but before they could act the underworld had warned the gang of the impending raid. Convinced that Ma's lover, Dunlop, had tipped off the police, the gang had him "rubbed out" and thereafter fled to Kansas City. They found a few recruits and with them robbed a bank, but the FBI picked up three of the hangers-on, and once again the Barkers fled.

Alvin Karpis   *Fred Barker*

Ma then turned her thoughts to her sons Arthur and Lloyd, languishing in jail, and began working to get them out. In 1932 "Doc" was released from Oklahoma State Penitentiary on condition that he leave the state, but Leavenworth could not be tampered with and Lloyd remained there. With "Doc" back in the gang, new bank robberies and murders took place and the mobsters moved on to Reno, St. Paul and Chicago. Bank robberies had now begun to pall, and Ma conceived the bigger idea of kidnaping. Their first victim was William A. Hamm, Jr., wealthy St. Paul brewer. On June 15, 1933, he was seized and taken to Illinois. Four days later he was released after $100,000 had been paid.

The gang then plotted the abduction of Edward G. Bremer, president of the Commercial State Bank of St. Paul. He was kidnaped January 17, 1934, taken to Illinois and held for three weeks. After payment of $200,000 ransom, he was released in Rochester, Minn., and the FBI moved in on the case. How the gang was tracked down is shown on the following pages.

Twenty-five members of the gang were convicted in connection with Bremer's abduction. There were six life imprisonments, three gangsters were killed while resisting arrest, and three were murdered by their fellow members. "Doc" Barker, sentenced to life imprisonment in Alcatraz, was killed in January, 1939, in an attempt to escape. Karpis, captured in New Orleans by Mr. Hoover and men of the FBI, is serving a life term in the same prison.

Ma Barker turned her home into a school for crime. As early as 1915 her boys were in trouble with the law, and many of their play-mates later became associated with them in crime. Here she looks on approvingly as two sons "mug" a young girl and snatch her purse.

On occasions when her sons were arrested for petty infractions of the law, Ma Barker would persuade the police to release them in her custody. Then she would upbraid the boys—not for the crime they had committed, but for being so stupid as to get caught. Ma's reputation spread, and her sons' gangster friends began to frequent the Barker home.

A few years later, Fred Barker (right) found himself in jail serving a sentence for burglary. While working in the prison bakery he met Alvin Karpis, who was to become one of the most dangerous of all gangsters. They stealthily talked of future crimes.

In solitary confinement for infractions of prison rules, Karpis determined to make his getaway. He sawed his way to freedom and fled to Chicago, where he joined the then powerful Barker gang.

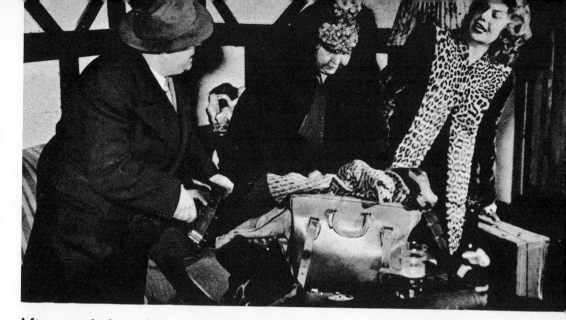

After murdering a Missouri sheriff, the gang took refuge in St. Paul, Minn. When members heard a police raid was imminent, Fred Barker, his mother and his "moll" packed hurriedly, sought a hideout.

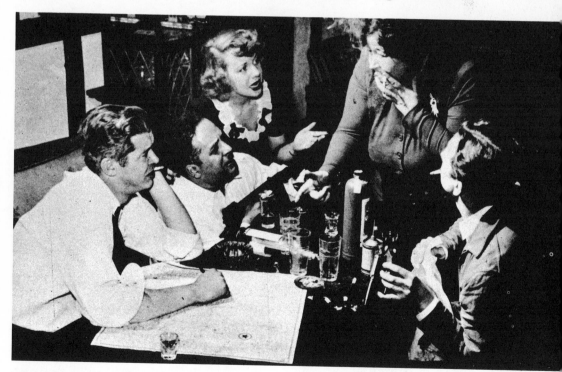

After kidnaping William A. Hamm, Jr., wealthy St. Paul brewer, and collecting $100,000 ransom, the gang planned to "snatch" Edward G. Bremer, St. Paul bank president. Here Karpis charts the getaway.

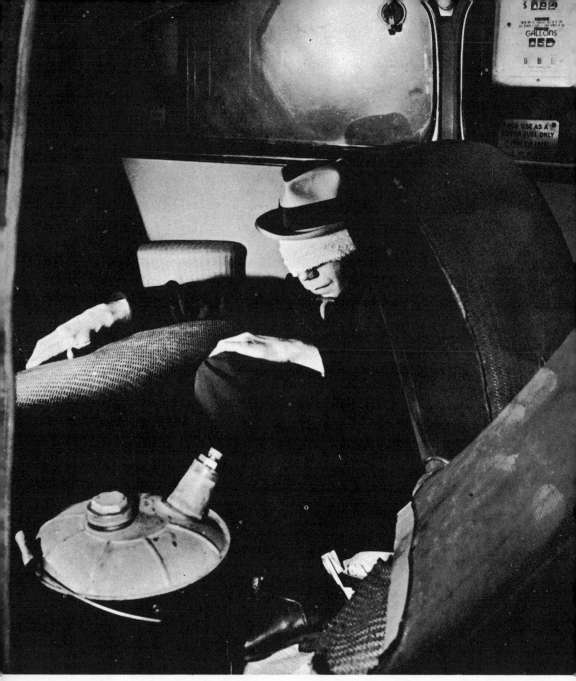

After payment of $200,000 ransom, Bremer was taken on a day-long trip from Bensenville, Ill., to Rochester, Minn., and was released there. Later he recalled that en route his abductors had filled the gas tank from an emergency can and then had thrown the can away. A farmer found it—after the FBI had put him on notice. Soon it was in the FBI laboratory. There a latent fingerprint was developed on the can; it was identified as Arthur Barker's.

136

With Bremer safe, the FBI began the hunt. Four flashlights used by the gang to give the pay-off signal were found and traced to a St. Paul store. A salesgirl identified a picture of Karpis as that of the man who had bought them. A nation-wide chase began .

With the proceeds of the Bremer kidnaping, Ma Barker had set herself up in a luxurious apartment on South Shore Drive, Chicago. She bought expensive furniture and clothing and indulged her taste for good living, meanwhile ruling over her boys with an iron hand.

More intelligent than any of her sons, she dominated them completely. Fred and Arthur especially were submissive to their strong-minded mother. She was bitterly jealous of their girl friends, and sometimes pushed them out of the gang's luxurious headquarters.

In a futile attempt to avoid identification, the Barker boys and Karpis were operated on by Dr. Joseph P. Moran, underworld surgeon, who tried unsuccessfully to alter their fingerprints and facial

characteristics. Here, suffering intense pain from these useless operations, they are being nursed by Ma and their "molls" at a home provided by Oliver A. Berg, a member of the gang.

But Dr. Moran drank too much, and when he drank he talked. He made the mistake of telling the gang he had them in the palm of his hand. So he was taken for a rowboat trip on Lake Erie—his last.

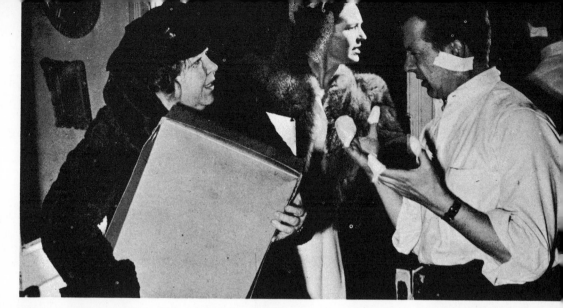

The ransom money was buried by one of the mobsters in a garage at Wilmington, Ill. When he was shot in a Cicero saloon, Ma and one of the girls recovered the cash, brought it to Chicago.

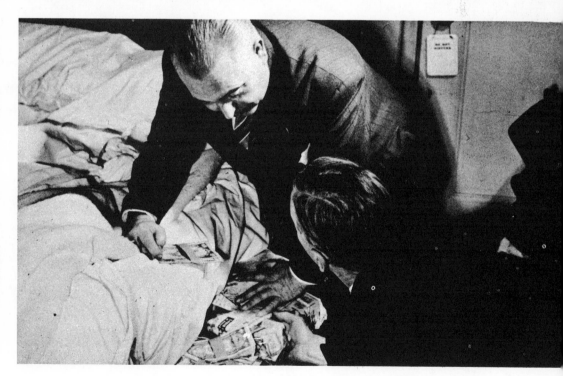

To get rid of the "hot" ransom money, the gang hired a Detroit gambler, who went to Havana and exchanged $72,000 in small bills. Above, he gets thousand-dollar bills from a broker.

143

FBI Agents trapped Russell (Slim) Gibson, one of the gang members, in his Chicago apartment. Gibson, wearing a bullet-proof vest, tried desperately to shoot his way out. But a G-Man's unerring aim was fatal, and the gangster fell on the stairway outside his door.

Arthur Barker was then trailed to his Chicago hideout and captured. When they searched him, the Agents found a map of Florida on which the town of Ocala was circled in pencil. With this clue they traced Ma and Fred Barker to a cottage by a lake near the town.

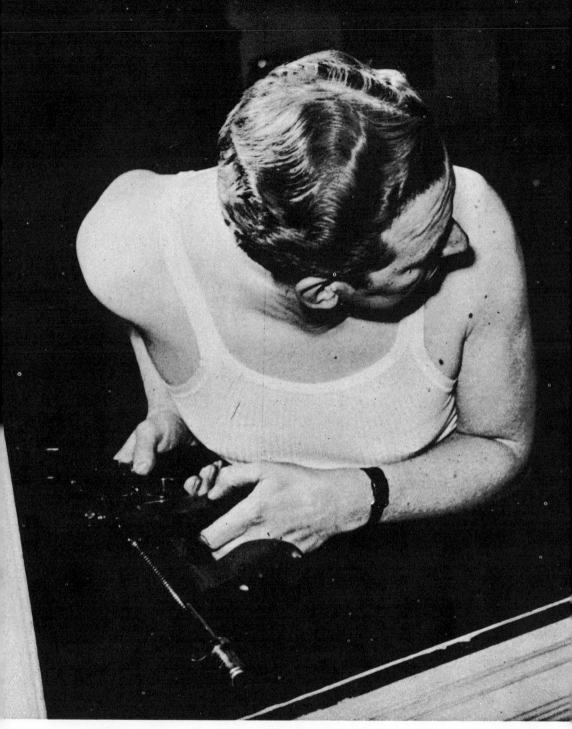

Their cottage surrounded by FBI Agents, Ma and Fred defied the command to come out with their hands up. They sent bursts of machine-gun fire from an upstairs window while the G-Men poured bullets and tear gas into every part of the frame dwelling. The battle

lasted nearly two hours, then the fire from the cottage ceased. Ma Barker's life of crime was at an end. With the capture of Alvin Karpis in New Orleans, the gang was eradicated at last. Three of her sons had been killed and the fourth was behind bars.

THE DOLL WOMAN

What was it that impelled Velvalee Dickinson to work for the Japs at the moment her country had its back to the wall? Was it misplaced loyalty or the $25,000 that changed hands? This native-born Californian and Stanford University graduate had been an enthusiastic member of the Japan-America Society in San Francisco since the early thirties. Her numerous Oriental friends included the confidential attache of the Japanese Consulate; she attended social gatherings at which members of the Japanese Navy and other high-ranking Japanese Government officials were present.

After being employed in the file department of a San Francisco bank, she entered a brokerage company in 1928. Until 1935 she was a bookkeeper in this business, operated by her husband. It handled many Japanese accounts in and around the city, and Mrs. Dickinson gained the reputation of being an excellent business woman. After this company went out of business, the couple came to New York in straitened circumstances in 1937. Velvalee obtained employment as a doll saleswoman in a department store and thereafter operated her own doll shop on Madison Avenue. There she catered to wealthy doll collectors and hobbyists interested in rare and expensive foreign, regional and antique dolls.

She found time, however, to visit the Nippon Club, the Japan Institute, and to cultivate the friendship of Kaname Wakasugi, the Japanese Consul General, and to meet Ichiro Yokoyama, the naval attache from Washington, D.C. These contacts were soon to pay off for the Japanese.

Velvalee Dickinson

Immediately after Pearl Harbor she began communicating to them vital information concerning fleet damage at Hawaii by means of letters addressed to a mail drop in Argentina. As return ad-

148

dresses on these letters she gave the names of several of her customers. Four of her letters came into the hands of the FBI through being returned from Argentina to the ostensible senders, marked "no such address." The language of these letters, couched in terms of the doll business, appeared peculiar and suspicious.

The letters were examined in the Laboratory. It was noted that the signatures were forgeries, prepared from original signatures in the possession of the forger. The typewriters used in their preparation were different in each case, but the typing characteristics showed that they were written by the same person. The dolls were described with reference to their nationalities and activities, the extent of repairs necessary and where these repairs were being made. FBI cryptographers concluded that an open code was being used, and that the letters conveyed information not of dolls but of the location, condition, damage and repair of U.S. naval vessels.

For instance, she wrote that she had three old china head dolls from England, which she had left for repair in a wonderful doll hospital. The FBI concluded correctly that these were three warships, and that the hospital was a shipyard where they were under repair. "I went to see Mr. Shaw. He destroyed your letter. You know he has been ill," she wrote in another communication. This letter was written shortly after it was known that the destroyer *Shaw*, which had its bow blown off at Pearl Harbor, was being repaired in a West Coast yard and would soon rejoin the fleet.

The women who had been drawn innocently into this spy plot by having their names and addresses signed to the letters turned the FBI's scrutiny on the dealer. Tracing her activities, Agents found that shortly after Pearl Harbor she had been in Seattle, San Francisco, New York, Portland and Oakland and again back in New York. After examining many specimens of her letters they came to the conclusion that she had used typewriters available to guests in West Coast hotels.

It was also discovered that this woman, who had continually borrowed small sums of money from banks and associates in New York as late as 1941, had an abnormal amount of hundred-dollar bills in 1943. Four bills which she used to pay debts were traced to Japanese official sources which had received the money before the war. After all possible information on the case had been developed, Special Agents arrested her in the New York bank vault where she kept her safe-deposit box.

In her smart Madison Avenue shop in New York City, Velvalee Dickinson appeared to deal exclusively in dolls. But back home in California she had been friendly with Japanese officials. Shortly before Pearl Harbor a Jap Embassy attache passed a code in her shop—and a roll of $25,000 in hundred-dollar bills.

After Pearl Harbor she made two trips to the West Coast and reported on damage and repairs to U.S. warships. She sent these reports to Señora Inez Lopez de Molinali in Buenos Aires, disguised
as letters about dolls, signed them with names of her customers and
put the return addresses of her customers on the envelopes.

One of the letters was undelivered in Argentina. It was returned to the "sender." Puzzled, the woman turned it over to the FBI. She said she had not written the letter, and had never known a Señora Molinali. When dolls were mentioned, she named several dealers she had done business with, including Mrs. Dickinson in New York . . .

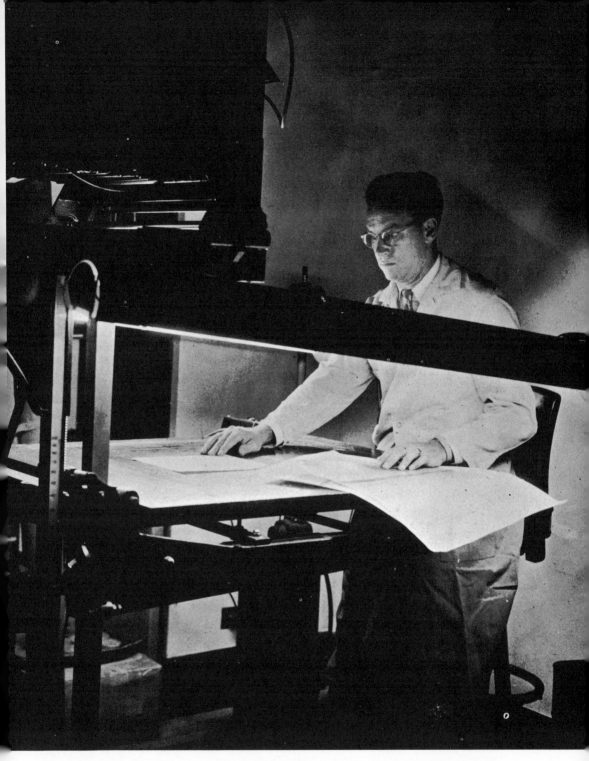

... and gave the Agent one of the doll woman's business letters. In the Laboratory, enlargements were made and it was compared with the Molinali letter. Both had been written on the same typewriter!

Other letters addressed to Señora Molinali began to turn up. With the postmarks as guides, Agents checked West Coast hotel registers and typewriters loaned to guests. Soon they had located the machines used by Velvalee Dickinson on her trips from New York.

With this evidence against her, Agents followed Mrs. Dickinson to a New York bank and arrested her as she opened her safe-deposit box. Of $15,000 in the box, $8,000 was later traced to Jap sources. The woman was sentenced to serve ten years and was fined $10,000.

THE HILLBILLY KILLER

Kinnie Wagner was a natural with guns. His skill as a trick-shot artist was widely known among the mountain people of southern Virginia ever since he had run away from home at the age of 17 to join a circus. He had thrilled his audiences for nearly three years by his feats. He could shoot the buttons off a man's vest; he would toss walnuts in the air and crack them with revolver shots. Perhaps it was his handiness with revolvers that led him into his lifetime of trouble. Some time in 1924 he had been in trouble with the law and had prudently retired to a cabin in Mississippi.

When a sheriff and three deputies approached on horseback to apprehend him on suspicion of robbery and jail-breaking, he bolted from the cabin. One of the deputies opened fire with a shotgun. The load caught Wagner along the belt line, smashing his revolver. He dashed back into the hut. Seizing his shotgun, he aimed through the window and fired both barrels point-blank at the approaching deputy. Escaping through the back door, he managed to reach his horse and made his escape. He had committed his first murder. His career as a killer had begun.

In the following year in Tennessee, he murdered two more officers who sought to arrest him. He gave himself up, was tried and sentenced to death. While awaiting execution, he engineered a dramatic jail break and escaped. But his guns, too hot for him, were burning holes in their holsters. In 1926 he killed two more men in a drunken quarrel in Arkansas and once more surrendered. He was turned over to Mississippi authorities and jailed for his first killing. Sentenced to life imprisonment, he remained docilely behind the bars for 14 years, and then made good his third prison break in 1940 as a trusty,

William Kenneth Wagner

156

after forcing a fellow guard to drive him some 40 miles.

In 1941 he headed back toward his birthplace in the mountain country of southwest Virginia, where he successfully eluded the authorities. Next year the FBI entered the case when a warrant was sworn out against him charging unlawful flight to escape prosecution for kidnaping the prison guard. The FBI carried on the manhunt for nine months. Wagner kept constantly changing his hiding place, a step ahead of the law. On one occasion, when he dropped in to see some friends he had known as a boy, he was wearing two .38 revolvers, a pistol similar to a Luger, a small-caliber revolver, a sawed-off shotgun and a full cartridge belt. The erstwhile trick-shot artist had become a walking arsenal.

When Special Agents and Virginia State Troopers finally caught up with him, as shown in the following pages, and lodged him in the Lynchburg jail, he talked freely of his life and outlook. It was his belief that a human being fights a losing battle from the moment he puts in an appearance on this earth. He claimed that Methuselah, who was said to have lived nearly 1,000 years, came nearer to winning the battle of life than anyone he had ever heard of, and that in the end he also lost.

When news of his capture reached the mountain folk, they were both relieved and saddened. At liberty, Kinnie Wagner had been a hillbilly Dillinger, but behind the bars he assumed some of the qualities of Robin Hood. On his arrest a flock of alleged relatives, including "wives," stormed the jail to see him. But Kinnie laughed them off, including the wives, declaring he had been too busy to get married. "They locked me up too soon and didn't give me a chance to do any courting," he said. Apparently he was introspective and occasionally pondered his life. While he was in jail he wrote the Special Agent in Charge at the Richmond office: "If everybody, I mean law, had been as nice as your branch of the service I can truthfully say I would not be in this trouble." Serving a life sentence in the Mississippi State Penitentiary, he occasionally sends a Christmas card to the Agents in Richmond. Although he no longer haunts the Appalachians, the memory of his smoking guns and stalwart figure is perpetuated by the mountain folk in the ballads they have composed about his sordid adventures.

The killer found himself in another gun battle in Tennessee in 1925. He wounded one policeman and killed a second and a deputy. He got away on horseback, evading the posse that was put on his trail by taking to a creek and swimming to the other side.

Exhausted after his swim, he begged shelter at the home of a widow. She let him sleep in her barn, and in the morning he told her he was the notorious Kinnie Wagner. She talked him into giving himself up. He did so and was sentenced to die for murder.

But the Blountville Jail did not hold him long. He escaped and, after a stay in Mexico, took a sawmill job near Texarkana, Ark. There he was soon in trouble again. A quarrel broke out and his

guns blazed once more. Two men lay dead when he stopped shooting. Something prompted him to give himself up to the sheriff. Mississippi claimed him for his first shooting, and he drew a life term.

After 14 years in prison, Wagner, then a trusty, helped guards track down escaped convicts. In 1940 he escaped again.

Later the FBI took up the chase, since Wagner had broken Federal laws. Meanwhile, Kinnie kept his shooting eye by constant practice.
162

By 1943 the hunt had narrowed to Scott County, Va., and in April Wagner was spotted riding in a car en route to Gate City. FBI men and Virginia State Troopers brought the car to a stop, but Wagner leaped into the tall grass at the roadside. A few minutes later he acknowledged his capture and was returned to prison in Mississippi.

THE INDIAN RESERVATION MURDERS

The Osage Indian country, in the northeastern part of Oklahoma, is a beautiful rolling country covered with tall green limestone grass; it is considered one of the finest cattle-grazing lands in the world. The Reservation, identical with Osage County, consists of 1,500,000 acres and contains more than 1,600 public schools. In 1907, head rights for 2,229 enrolled members of the Osage Tribe were created. This number of head rights remains stationary, although the actual number of the tribe may vary, and the Indians draw revenue from or are allotted tracts of land based upon their head rights. The original allotment to each Indian was 160 acres and a homesite, which was subsequently added to until each head right allotment consisted of approximately 657 acres.

At the beginning of the century, each Indian entitled to receive income from the common fund was drawing about $200 annually. When oil was struck on the Reservation near the end of the first decade of the century, the fortunes of the Indians changed overnight. The net per capita payments increased enormously. By the early twenties, each Osage Indian was getting $12,400 annually. By 1931 the 2,000 Indians who had enjoyed head rights since the discovery of oil had been paid a total net revenue of $241,546,290. They were thus enormously wealthy, and they were exceedingly profligate with their money. Those who were deemed able to handle their own affairs were permitted to dispose of their funds as they saw fit. It was not uncommon from 1920 to 1925 for the grocery bills of numerous Indians to run from $500 to $1,000 each per month.

Osage County and the surrounding territory contain very wild stretches of country, affording excellent concealment in thickly wooded tracts and almost inaccessible canyons. At the time of the murders, from 1921 to 1923, the country was a haven for all types of desperate criminals, attracted both by the hiding places and the enormous wealth of the Osage Indians. One bandit serving time in the Oklahoma State Penitentiary told Special Agents that during this period he attended a gathering of thirty-two nationally known bank bandits and train robbers, all fugitives from justice, at which they spent most of their time in pistol practice. One notorious bad-

164

man, Henry Grammer, had complete control of the Osage liquor traffic and was reputed to work a gang of criminals, who had fled from all over the United States, day and night in making illicit liquor. Grammer was killed in what looked like an automobile accident; a notorious bandit was with him at the time of the mishap, and Grammer had a gaping wound under his left armpit. There was no investigation. The local authorities apparently approved of his death.

Before the tribe got rich overnight through the discovery of oil, William K. Hale, sometimes called "King of the Osage," drifted into the country from Texas. He was an uneducated and more or less uncouth cowpuncher and cattle thief, but he had a domineering personality. He grew wealthy in his dealings with the Indians, eventually becoming a millionaire who dominated local politics and who seemingly could not be punished for the many crimes that were laid at his door.

Greedy for more wealth, Hale schemed to get his hands on the large fortune of an Indian family by the name of Kile. The mother, Lizzie Kile, had four daughters, Mollie, Anna, Rita and Minnie. Mollie was the wife of Hale's nephew, Ernest Burkhart. Hale determined to murder the whole family—Mollie's sisters and mother first, so that Mollie would inherit the estate, and then Mollie, so that his nephew would be the sole heir. Hale knew that he could persuade Ernest to cooperate with him.

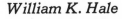

John Ramsey   *William K. Hale*

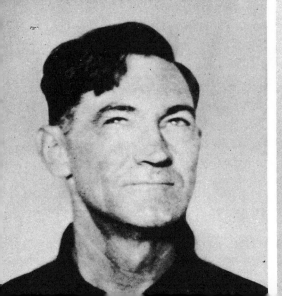

By 1921 Hale had succeeded in leasing 45,000 acres of Indian land and had acquired a bank, a store partnership and political power.

In May, Anna was shot and rolled into a ravine near Fairfax, Okla., by two men hired by Hale. Within a year, Anna's mother and sister Minnie died natural deaths. Now only two sisters stood between Hale and the Kile family fortune.

In 1922, at a bandits' convention in the Osage Hills where criminals from all over the nation gathered, he asked Henry Grammer, boot-
168

leg king, to find him a man to kill two relatives of the Kile family.
For the job Grammer picked John Ramsey, a cattle rustler.

Ramsey murdered Henry Roan, an Indian who had become suspicious of Hale, and two months later touched off a keg of nitroglycerin that blew up Rita's home in Fairfax, killing Rita, her husband and a servant. In this crime he was accompanied by Ace Kirby. Hale, with the Kile fortune almost in his grasp, now began to fear that Kirby would betray him. Setting a trap for Kirby, he told him that the owner of a grocery store near the Kansas-Oklahoma state line kept some valuable jewels on the premises and urged him to steal them. Then Hale approached the owner of the store and warned him that he was about to be robbed.

When Kirby broke into the store he was met by a rain of buckshot.
Relieved of a possible informer, Hale turned to Mollie Burkhart.

It was learned that Mollie was slowly dying from what was believed
to be poisoning. After she was removed from the influence of Hale's
cohorts, she completely regained her health.

Other Osage Indians died under mysterious circumstances. After being plied with liquor, they were examined by a doctor who pronounced them intoxicated and gave them morphine. When he had left, a second and lethal dose of morphine was injected. The death certificate read "death from alcoholic poisoning."

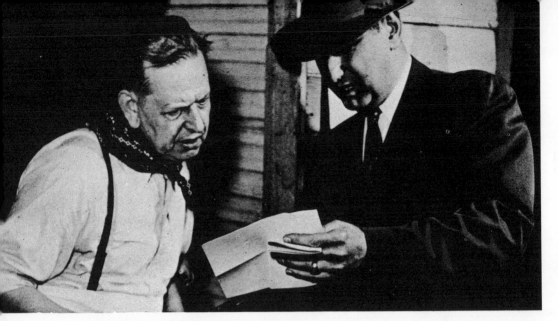

The tribe petitioned the Government for aid. The FBI went into action. One Agent adopted the role of insurance salesman; another posed as a medicine man and joined in the tribe's ceremonials.

A third became a Texas cowman to enable him to get in touch with Hale's intimates and relatives. It took three years to complete the case against Hale and his associates in mass murder.

174

But when the case was turned over to the state, Hale and his gang were given life imprisonment. Their job done, the Agents unmasked and the Osage chief inscribed his gratitude in the tribal records.

THE BRADY GANG

The Brady Gang, which for two years left a red-hot trail of robberies, holdups and murders behind it, was a first-class example of how criminals get that way, how they start out into trouble, and how they stay with it.

Alfred Brady had been orphaned at 16. He soon discovered, to his discomfiture, that to make money he would have to work, but he didn't like work. By 1934 he ought to have found out that easy money doesn't pay off. He was arrested on a charge of possessing stolen property and was sentenced to serve 180 days on an Indiana state farm. But the only lessons he learned from this experience were those taught him by the other inmates. He boned up on crime techniques at the feet of masters, and determined not to mend his ways but to become a better criminal. On his release in 1935, he met James Dalhover.

At the age of 11, Dalhover had been sent to reform school with his older brother George for robbing an Indiana country grocery store. Released in 1918 after sixteen months, he continued his grammar school education in Cincinnati. He married at 19 and spent the next year making illicit liquor. Caught in that same year, 1925, with his brother George and a load of moonshine in Kentucky, he was sentenced to a hundred-day jail term and paid a $100 fine.

He and his brother tolerated the jail only three weeks. Then they broke out and headed for Arizona. They stole a car in New Mexico. There the law caught up with them and sentenced them to spend two years in the New Mexico State Penitentiary. Paroled after thirteen months, they were returned to Kentucky where they were sentenced to two years for assault

Clarence Lee Shaffer

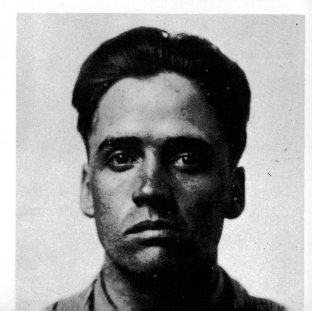

176

with intent to kill, a small matter incident to their escape from jail.

When Jimmy Dalhover was released, he headed back home to Cincinnati, where he did odd jobs. But not for long. That old liquor business kept beckoning. Soon he was back making moonshine, with easy profits. By 1933 he had done so well that he bought a farm in Indiana. Did he settle down to a quiet farming life? He merely got into the liquor business on a bigger and better scale. In 1935 he met Al Brady, when Brady was turned loose from the state farm. During the following week they met Clarence Shaffer.

Shaffer, like his new-found pals, was also the product of a misspent youth. He was born in Indianapolis in 1916, and was just 21 when he made his last mistake—trying to shoot it out with FBI men. At 12, he was stripping and stealing automobiles. When he met Brady and Dalhover in October, 1935, he was a cocky 19-year-old petty thief who bragged about a fancied relationship with Dillinger, who had been exterminated the year before.

By this time gangsterism was at low ebb. Dillinger, Nelson and Karpis had already passed into history and had left a bad taste behind them. The days of gangster worship were over. Harboring criminals was a Federal offense, and those likely to be guilty of it had been well warned by the FBI. The Bureau, in fact, had made life exceedingly difficult for big-time criminals. But the Brady gang, young and brash, had not yet learned this. They were determined to become the new career men of the underworld. They laid their plans and tried their luck at robbing stores every Saturday night.

James Dalhover   *Alfred Brady*

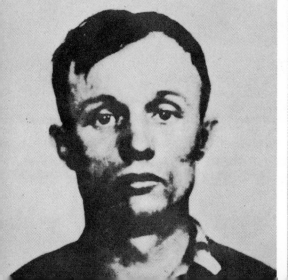

Then the three hoodlums began a series of robberies designed to make Dillinger look like a piker. Alfred Brady, James Dalhover and Clarence Shaffer started with gas stations and drugstores.

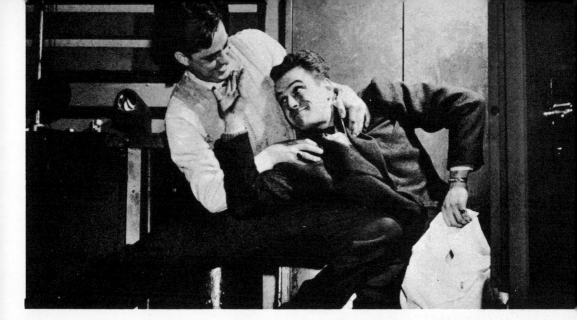

While Brady was rifling the safe of a Lima, Ohio, jewelry store in 1936, an employee jumped on him. He freed himself and fled with his gang, carrying the loot in pillow cases—$6,800 in jewelry.

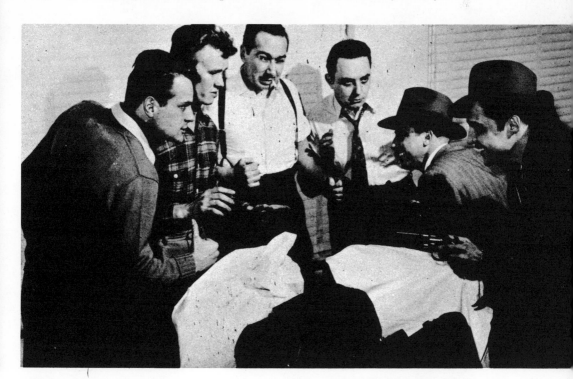

Three weeks later the trio took $27,000 worth of jewels from a Dayton store and agreed to sell them to Chicago fences for $22,000. But a gang of thugs at the rendezvous relieved them of the loot.

Back to the Lima store went the trio for another haul. When they emerged, they found a police car parked in front of their own. They shot it out with the police and made their getaway successfully.

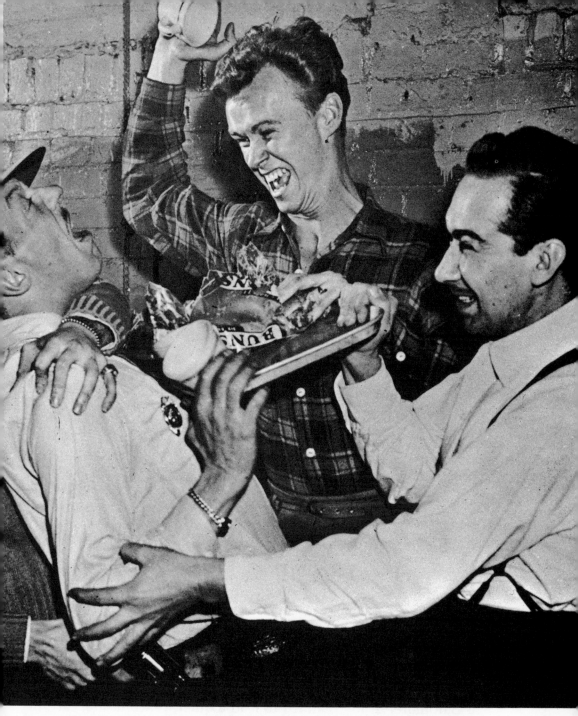

In another battle in Indianapolis, the Brady gang killed a policeman. Rounded up, they were lodged in an Indiana jail. One morning they assaulted the sheriff as he brought their breakfast, seized his gun, shot their way out of jail, stole a car and headed for Baltimore. The FBI took up their trail for Federal offenses.

In Baltimore, Brady planned to lead a quiet, peaceful life, carrying out his robberies far away. Dalhover and Shaffer married sisters under assumed names, and the girls often went roller skating with the gang. The mobsters were now holding up banks, and to explain their absences, they told the girls they had to travel to Maine to attend to a furniture business they owned there.

In 1937, after robbing an Indiana bank, the trio ambushed a state policeman and a deputy sheriff who had pursued them to a church. In the battle an officer was killed. Once more the gang fled north.

The Brady gang's members were so fond of guns they even stole them from American Legion monuments. They ordered a machine gun from a Maine sports store, saying they would call for it. When Dalhover arrived for the gun, FBI men arrested him.

But Shaffer came in shooting from his post outside the door when he saw the Agents nab Dalhover. He wounded one Agent in the shoulder. The FBI men returned his fire and he turned and ran into the street, where he fell and died a few minutes later, gun in hand.

Meanwhile Brady leaped from the car with gun in action, but two Agents closed in on him, and Brady fell beside his companion. Dal-

186

hover was electrocuted in Indiana. In its career of crime the gang
had committed nearly 150 holdups and had killed several men.

THE DILLINGER CASE

On May 10, 1933, one John Herbert Dillinger was paroled from the Indiana State Prison after serving more than eight and a half years for assault and battery with intent to rob. He was comparatively unknown to law enforcement officers; the people of the United States had never heard of him.

Fourteen months later he was killed while resisting arrest. News of his death was broadcast immediately and the press played up the end of his sensational career. For in that brief period he had become the country's most notorious and highly publicized outlaw, a man whose name was familiar to everyone. Movies were based on his life, and an inglorious career of crime was treated like a saga of heroism and daring. He had committed major offenses, mostly bank robberies, in more than half-a-dozen Midwestern states, and his apprehension was sought in virtually every section of the country.

Following his release on parole, bank robberies began happening in Ohio, Michigan, Indiana and Illinois in which Dillinger and associates were believed to have participated. In September, 1933, he was arrested in Dayton, Ohio, and was committed to the county jail at Lima to await trial for the robbery of a bank at Bluffton. He had not long to wait before his friends of the underworld sprang him out of that predicament.

One October evening three men entered the sheriff's office. They said they were from the Indiana State Prison and had come to get Dillinger, a parolee from that institution. When the sheriff asked for their credentials, he was shot and beaten. The dying man's keys were removed and Dillinger was liberated.

Again the incidence of bank robbery soared. In some

John Dillinger

188

cases there was definite proof that Dillinger was a member of the gang. It was known that he twice robbed police departments in Indiana a few days after his escape, obtaining machine guns, rifles and revolvers, ammunition and bullet-proof vests. In January, 1934, the gang robbed the First National Bank of East Chicago, Indiana, and killed a police officer at the bank. They hastened to Florida, where they spent a few days before starting out for the Pacific Coast. In Tucson, Arizona, Dillinger and three others were arrested by the local police; they had more than $25,000 in their possession and carried a veritable arsenal of arms and ammunition.

Dillinger was returned to Indiana, where he was committed to the county jail at Crown Point. In March he subdued his guards, liberated another prisoner awaiting trial for murder, and escaped by stealing the sheriff's automobile, which he abandoned in Chicago, thus violating the National Motor Vehicle Theft Act and bringing himself at last within the jurisdiction of the FBI. The Bureau immediately filed a complaint against him and a warrant was issued, although it was realized that the State authorities had a better claim against him if he were apprehended, since he was wanted for murder and numerous bank robberies. Every Field Office was quick to pursue any probable leads in its district; the names of Dillinger's relatives, friends and contacts were obtained and they were placed under surveillance. His photograph, fingerprints, description and record were furnished to every law enforcement agency in the United States.

On the last day of March, in St. Paul, Minn., he escaped from Agents after a gun battle in which he received a bullet wound in the leg. He was treated by a Minneapolis physician, and then hurried to his father's home in Mooresville, Indiana. In April he was traced to Sault Sainte Marie, then to a resort near Rhinelander, Wisconsin, where he once more made his escape after a gunfight. In the course of this episode a Special Agent was killed and another was wounded by Lester M. Gillis, alias Baby Face Nelson, one of Dillinger's associates. The search went on unrelentingly, resulting in the arrest of several other wanted criminals in no way related to the fugitive.

By July the hunt had narrowed to the Chicago area. Many of Dillinger's friends had been apprehended on harboring and other charges, and the chase had become so hot he was forced to lie low.

In May, 1934, when he was hiding in Chicago, Dillinger picked up
Polly Hamilton, a sandwich shop waitress, in a Wilson Avenue saloon. The two became friendly and arranged to meet the next day.

Two days later she brought him to the apartment of a friend, Anna Sage, who recognized Dillinger, but peace was made between the trio.

Two months later, facing deportation for immoral activities, Anna Sage met an FBI man through an East Chicago, Indiana, police officer and told him that she could lead him to Dillinger.

The next night, two Agents in an FBI car near the Biograph Theater saw Dillinger arrive with the two women. As prearranged, Anna Sage wore a red dress. The trap was set.

One Agent was posted near the theater entrance, two in a doorway and one in a car. Other FBI men under Inspector Sam Cowley, who had been put in charge of the case by Director Hoover, and East Chicago, Indiana, police officers were stationed across the street.

When Dillinger emerged with the woman in the red dress, the Agent at the door lit his cigar, the signal of recognition.

As the three walked out of the theater, two Agents fell in behind and others immediately began to close slowly from all sides. Dillinger suddenly sensed a trap. As he came abreast of the car, he shoved the women behind him and peered closely at the occupant.

Ignoring a command to surrender, he whipped out his gun and headed for an alley. Other Agents had already closed it off, but Dillinger was determined to shoot it out. He fell at last in the gutter, making good his boast that he "would never be taken alive."

Chapter IV

How the FBI Helped Win World War II

In the first World War the FBI was one of several agencies investigating wartime violations. There were about 20 different Federal Agencies, hastily recruited and lacking training and coordination; their activities were confused and overlapping. Vigilante groups and many untrained and irresponsible people undid much of the good work of private citizens aiding the Government, and this resulted in misdirected effort, witch hunts, dragnet raids and mob hysteria. When the first World War came to an end, a limited number of statutes pertaining to espionage and sabotage remained in the jurisdiction of the FBI.

During the thirties, when the Bureau's new authority and powers were enabling it to clean up the gangsters at home, information concerning foreign gangsters who were beginning to operate on an international scale started to flow into the files. Subversive movements began to attract official attention. In 1933 an investigation of National Socialist activities was made. The German-American Bund, which developed from organizations formed before Hitler came to power, had begun to infiltrate ever more boldly into the lives of German communities throughout the nation, and the Bureau had compiled by this time an impressive file on Nazis in America. Ironically enough, however, the first official probe of the Nazis grew out of a request by the State Department to investigate a threat to kill Hitler.

In 1938–39, when the pattern of Nazi world hegemony had become plain for all to see, the Bureau began compiling information on German aliens. In appropriation hearings about that time, Director Hoover disclosed to the House committee what was being done, with the result that a clamor arose from some liberal and left-wing groups, charging a threat to the civil liberties of these persons.

In the summer of 1939, President Roosevelt sent a confidential directive to the Army and Navy Intelligence services and the FBI placing the responsibility with regard to espionage, counterespionage and sabotage on these three agencies; the FBI was designated the central clearing house of all law enforcement bodies and was put in charge of national defense activities insofar as they involved civilians. In September of the same year, the President issued another directive calling on all law enforcement agencies to report directly to the FBI any information relating to espionage, counterespionage, sabotage, subversive activities and neutrality violations. Thus the FBI shouldered the heaviest responsibility in its history—the task of protecting the internal security of the nation from foreign enemies.

It was known that German agents were being trained, and a wave of spying and sabotage was expected; thousands of enemies were already within the United States awaiting the day of attack. But the FBI was already spying on the spy. Files grew bulkier as the mass of information on actual and potential enemies increased. The general policy was necessarily one of watchful waiting. The Bureau's task was to identify enemy agents, keep them under 24-hour surveillance and, by allowing them to lead the Agents to other spies, to incriminate as many as possible. If the Bureau showed its hand at any moment, the situation might blow up. The task had to be done on a national basis with the cooperation of local law enforcement officials and private citizens. "Don't investigate anything yourself," became the prime instruction to Americans. "Report it to the FBI." In one day 2,800 reports of suspicious happenings were received. Many of them were foolish imaginings; many were spiteful tales concocted in malice against neighbors, employers and fellow workers. They all had to be considered and investigated if they appeared specific.

Defense work poured into the Bureau and its Field Offices in flood proportions. Potentially dangerous aliens were identified and placed under scrutiny. Such investigations by the FBI were designed primarily to prepare for the day when a real emergency would come in protecting the nation's security; but they also removed unfounded suspicions from loyal aliens. All applicants for positions in war industries were fingerprinted. The Identification Division found its work increased sevenfold as millions of cards came streaming into its files from all over the country. The pre-emergency identification file contained 11,000,000 cards; now there are more than 132,000,-000 fingerprints on record. The War Department alone poured 17,500,000 cards into the files, the Navy 4,000,000, the Civil Service 8,000,000, and the Alien Registration 5,000,000.

With its work increased so many times over, the need for additional personnel was imperative. At this time there were 851 Special Agents. By 1943 there were approximately 5,000. They were trained by the most intensive methods the FBI ever used. A new class of Agents began each Monday and worked each day from 9 A.M. to 9 P.M. for four months. A new barracks was built at Quantico, Virginia, to accommodate the men the FBI needed so badly. New Field Offices were opened by the Bureau in Honolulu, Puerto Rico and Alaska.

In 1939 the War and Navy Departments requested the FBI to conduct surveys of key war production plants. The most important plants in the country were toured in a study of their layout and protective devices; in all, some 2,350 plants were surveyed. A training course on plant survey methods was inaugurated. Agents were assigned to this course and were then sent to the Field Offices. The sole purpose of the Bureau in this matter was to investigate and improve protective devices; it took no part in labor and personnel relations.

In this survey plan, American industry was most cooperative. Before the war began major war plants had been completed and industry had spent literally millions putting the FBI recommendations into effect to make their plants spy-proof and sabotage-proof. Astounding discoveries were made, however, illustrating how American business men little realized the threat of sabotage that loomed as war came to these shores. Here are a few examples of what the Special Agents found on the early visits:

The guards were frequently old men, pensioners, employed as watchmen. The plants were virtually unguarded and easy to get into. One Agent walked through the main entrance of a plane plant into the drafting room and questioned the men there about their work—all without being hindered. In another plant the front entrance was found to be secure, but at the rear a wooden door fastened only by a wooden turn button led directly into the boiler room. There were plants where the linen covering on fire hose had rotted and was incapable of standing pressure, and where water buckets for fire fighting hung on the walls but had no bottoms in them.

In one plant manufacturing airplane and marine engines for the U.S. Army and Navy, and holding a large contract with the British Government, the Agent was told that it was adequately supplied with vault and safe space for confidential plans and blueprints. The officials proudly displayed these safes in the tool design and engineering departments. You can imagine their embarrassment and the G-Man's amazement when he found that the combination of each safe was plainly printed on the door beneath the lock. In another plant, one vault containing plans entrusted to the company by the War and Navy Departments had an imposing fire-proof door, but the walls had wooden partitions. Another was so constructed that the rear wall was a window looking out and giving access to the street. None of the plant executives had noticed these conditions until they were pointed out by the FBI men. Another plant, working on a jet propulsion plane highly secret at the time, kept the model enclosed by a wall of cardboard in which a workman had kicked a hole large enough to walk through.

Beginning his survey of one plant, a Special Agent entered each of its three gates in succession without being questioned, although he wore no identifying badge. Then he toured the factory, mingling with workmen and technicians. He poked around among highly confidential activities, asking questions and receiving courteous replies. Needless to say, this plant later instituted a system of identification and investigation of its employees. Another Agent was advised by plant officials that applicants for employment were investigated before being engaged. The officials were considerably surprised to learn that the Agent had ascertained that an individual had worked in the engine room—a vital point—for three days before it was discovered that he was insane and had been discharged from his previous place of employment for that reason.

Another company engaged in developing a robot pilot kept the plans and records of more than five years of experimentation, as well as the working model, in a flimsy single-story building. The entire fire-fighting apparatus protecting these irreplaceable records and the model consisted of two carbon tetrachloride extinguishers and the workers had got into the habit of washing their hands with the filler, a good solvent for grease.

By the time war came to the United States, the great factories turning out planes, tanks, ships and guns no longer stood open and unprotected; American industry was fully conscious of the threat to national safety. So well had the FBI done its work and so thoroughly had industry cooperated in its preparedness program that not one case of enemy-directed sabotage came to light during the war, although thousands of cases of reported sabotage were investigated. In almost every instance, they were found to be accidents or acts committed by pranksters or soreheads. Some of the horseplay that went on in American war plants was almost incredible; the hours of production that were lost through sheer tomfoolery were staggering.

In one New York City plant, work shoes were nailed to the floor, work clothes were hidden, machinery parts were spot-welded to the floor, screws were removed from the work benches of fellow employees so that the benches fell to pieces when opened. In other plants throughout the country stink bombs, itching powder and fake infernal machines made their appearance with painful regularity. Drinking on the job was accomplished by mixing liquor and soft drinks and keeping the bottle openly on the bench. Workmen playfully pitched nuts and bolts at each other; occasionally the gadgets fell into the machinery, and an expensive machine was out of commission for hours. It is hard to understand how a lampshade could find its way into a $20,000 drill press until it is explained that one workman first put it on the head of another. The "hot foot" was a perennial delight of war plant employees, and at least one man died when his work clothes, impregnated with oil and grease, flared up when this trick was played on him.

All these cases had to be investigated by the FBI in time-consuming examination. They were acts of thoughtlessness and stupidity, but they were as much a hindrance to war production as if they had been committed by enemy agents. The enemy agent, however, was conspicuously unsuccessful in sabotaging American industry in the second World War. There were no major acts of sabotage comparable to the great Kingsland fire or the Black Tom explosion in the first World War.

But the enemy was not asleep. He had built up in the United States an organization of friends—Americans of German birth,

American-born citizens of German descent, and German aliens—all conspiring against America in the interests of the fatherland. The FBI was to be embroiled with these people in the deadliest struggle ever waged to protect the internal security of the nation. In that battle the Bureau was aided by its years of preparation, by its experiences in the first World War, by its unsleeping watch over the enemy within the gates, and, at last, by the hand of fate that with one gesture bared the secrets of the Reich's espionage system. The tale is strange and engrossing.

In the Imperial German Army of 1914–1918, in which Adolf Hitler served as a corporal, there was a private who was to become Hitler's nemesis in the United States. Tiring of impoverished Germany in 1921, the man who had once been a private went to sea, came to America and subsequently worked in various industrial and airplane engineering plants. In 1936 he became a naturalized American citizen.

Three years later he returned to his birthplace, Mülheim in the Ruhr, to visit his mother. The moment he stepped from the gangplank in Hamburg the hand of the Gestapo reached out and clapped him on the shoulder. A plain-clothes official questioned him about his employment in the United States and dismissed him with the ominous phrase: "You will wait to hear from us in the near future." Deeply troubled, he continued his journey to Mülheim, where he found employment with the Sieman Schukert Company, engaged in the construction of steam turbines under consignment from Westinghouse Electric in the United States.

Several months passed, until one day he received a letter advising him that the writer, a Dr. Gassner, had a matter of importance to discuss with him. The half-forgotten Hamburg warning came back full force. Puzzled and resentful, he took the letter to the local Gestapo headquarters, where he was told that it would be advisable to see this Dr. Gassner.

Around September 1, 1939, Dr. Gassner visited him in Mülheim and attempted to gain information concerning planes and equipment in the United States. At the end of this interview, the doctor requested him to return to America to act as an espionage agent for "unsere Gesellschaft"—"our organization." The American realized that he was in the hands of the Gestapo, but he did not commit himself, pleading that he needed time to think things over. The Gestapo did not intend to give him time. Returning to his hotel

202

shortly after the occasion of Dr. Gassner's visit, he discovered that his U.S. passport had been stolen.

Again Gassner came to call on him, this time fortified with the presence of a Dr. Renken, later discovered to be none other than Major Nickolaus Ritter, of the German Secret Service, one of the men who was charged with directing the activities of German agents abroad. (As a matter of fact, Major Ritter had lived in the vicinity of New York City as Nikki Ritter for three years in the guise of a textile engineer and had returned to Germany in 1937 on a mission for the German Intelligence Service. But it was hopeless to try to make the American people believe that there could be such a thing as German spies in their midst. In peacetime? Nonsense! Just the FBI having nightmares!)

Between them, Gassner and Ritter broke down the American citizen's unwillingness to comply with their plans. Their method was simplicity itself: they threatened reprisals on his family in Germany unless he became an espionage agent for the Reich. Since his maternal grandfather was a Jew, our man realized that he had better fall in with their plans.

However, he had plans of his own. At the American Consulate in Cologne, where he applied for a new passport to replace the stolen one, he secretly let his fellow Americans know that he was returning to the United States to spy for Hitler and that he wanted the FBI to make contact with him when he got there. Next he reported to Ritter in Hamburg to be trained for his work. He became Harry Sawyer, the name by which he was to be known in the United States.

He was housed in a pension in the Klopstockstrasse operated by a German couple and their daughter as a training barracks for German agents who were being prepared for assignment throughout the world, and there, in an atmosphere of silent mistrust and suspicion, where no one spoke more than a few words, he began his training for the deadly work he was supposed to do.

His mentor at the Klopstock pension was Hugo Sebold, otherwise Heinrich Sorau, head of Nazi espionage training. From him he learned how to prepare coded messages, how to use a Leica camera for the preparation of microphotographs of documents, plans and maps, how to send by radio transmitter. He was instructed to get in touch with an amateur radio operator in the United States, so that he could establish short-wave communication with the Reich. He was told to join the National Guard to obtain information concerning arms and equipment. His instructions were to send all the data he could regarding ship movements, military establishments, war production, new developments, production of military aircraft, the training of Air Corps personnel and flying schools, and the progress of heavy water experimentation—already the Germans suspected the atomic bomb. To enable him to transmit this information, he was supplied with a five-letter transposition code, the key to which was the novel popular at that time, *All This and Heaven, Too.*

When his training was complete, Sawyer was given several microphotographs to conceal in the back of his watch. Two of these were to be retained by him, since they contained detailed instructions. Three others were to be delivered to Colonel Fritz Duquesne, 17 East 42nd Street; Lilly Stein, 127 East 54th Street, New York City; and Everett Roeder, 210 Smith Street, Merrick, Long Island. Sawyer was also instructed to reach Herman Lang in Glendale, Long Island. He was given $1,000 in American currency, $500 of which was to be given to Roeder, the remainder to be used for expenses and the purchase of a Leica camera. With addresses in China, Brazil and Portugal to be used as letter drops, Sawyer was ready to leave. He bade farewell to his superiors, and as a parting joke, told them he hoped to send the details of the Norden bomb sight. They smiled cryptically. Sawyer was later to learn that the secret of the existence of the Norden bomb sight had long been in the hands of the Nazis, transmitted by one of the very men he had been instructed to see!

He arrived in New York on February 8, 1940. He was met immediately by FBI Agents. To them he redeclared his loyal intentions to cooperate with them as a bona fide representative of the German spy organization and help them to ferret out the identities of other spies operating in the United States. In accordance with Hugo Sebold's instructions, he cabled: "Arrived safe. Had pleasant trip," meaning that he was free of surveillance and was ready to start work.

Sawyer rented office space in West 42nd Street, where he posed as a consulting Diesel engineer. The FBI had previously arranged for this when they rented the adjoining suite of offices. Sawyer's office was wired for sound and an X-ray mirror was installed in the wall between the two offices. Thus visual, microphonic and photographic surveillance of every meeting held in Sawyer's office was maintained by FBI Agents. Here his various aides were to meet him and were to be observed in action as they brought information, demanded pay for their work and incriminated themselves as agents of the German Reich before the hidden cameras and recording machines.

A short-wave radio transmitting station was erected and operated by Agents of the FBI at Centerport, Long Island. It maintained practically daily communication with Hamburg, sending the information garnered by Sawyer from his aides after it had been passed on by War and Navy Intelligence and the FBI, and details of a confidential nature had been deleted. Occasionally, false information was inserted in these messages to confuse the enemy still further without arousing his suspicions. By June, 1941, 296 radio messages had been sent to the Nazi spy command and 165 had been received from Hamburg.

What was the connection between Fritz Duquesne, Lily Stein, Everett Roeder and Herman Lang and the German espionage system? That was the first question the FBI wanted an answer to as Harry Sawyer sat back in his new office and prepared to go to work on the gang. How many more were there, spreading through the ranks of engineers, waiters, stewards, defense plant workers and seamen? Ensconced in his office, Sawyer was soon to provide the key. Shortly German agents were to come streaming in, constantly under the surveillance of the FBI, handing over information, demanding payment, complaining of the little money they got.

The most colorful figure and the biggest fish among them was Frederick Joubert Duquesne, the first associate Sawyer acquired. Intrigue, sabotage and espionage had been his business since the days of the Boer War. He had become a naturalized American citizen in 1913. In 1916, the British steamship *Tennyson* caught fire and sank on the high seas. The fire had originated in boxes labeled "minerals," shipped to New York from Brazil by Duquesne. He attempted to collect insurance for this loss, claiming that his boxes contained ores and motion picture film. As a result of these and other claims against insurance companies, he was charged with fraud about the same time that the British Government sought his extradition on charges of murder and attempting to sink and destroy the *Tennyson*. With the adroitness that characterized his later career, Duquesne pleaded guilty to the fraud charge, interposed a plea of insanity, got himself committed to Bellevue Hospital and escaped by sawing through the window bars and scaling a six-foot wall and a seven-foot spiked fence.

When Sawyer got back to New York in 1940, Duquesne was doing business as "Air Terminals Company" at 120 Wall Street. Sawyer communicated with him by letter and later called on him at his office. Duquesne greeted him briefly and immediately handed him a slip of paper reading, "We will go out. Cannot talk here." Duquesne proved to be extremely cautious about conducting conversations; he appeared to be constantly apprehensive about surveillance and took remarkable. pains to throw would-be followers off his track. One of his favorite tricks was to board a subway train, stand near the door, and just as the doors were about to close, jump out. At their first meeting, he and Sawyer repaired to an automat, where they talked in somewhat general terms until Duquesne mentioned that he had received a letter "from China," meaning one of the letter drops through which mail passed to and from spies. With this as common ground, the two men exchanged information concerning various members of the German espionage system with whom they had been in contact. Thereafter Duquesne was a frequent visitor to Sawyer's office in 42nd Street. When Sawyer delivered the microphotograph to him, he appeared to be thoroughly familiar with it as a means of conveying information.

Duquesne gave Sawyer numerous items of information on defense materials for transmission to Germany. On one occasion, with elaborate caution, he withdrew a paper containing information from one of his socks, while the FBI movie camera secretly recorded the scene. Technical data, ship movements, national defense information were Duquesne's metier. He told Sawyer he had sent a new type of American gas mask to Germany through Italy, thus revealing the existence of a courier system at the disposal of this spy ring. Later the couriers themselves were to enter Sawyer's office and incriminate themselves.

They were a curious lot, these men in the pay of a foreign power. The movies taken show them in their true colors—boastful, crafty, sly, suspicious, avaricious and sometimes stupid. They would seat themselves in the chair provided for them—directly opposite the X-ray mirror on the wall—and with expansive gesture and cunning grimace recount their exploits, in which they had all the brains and the dumb Americans had none. Once Duquesne showed Sawyer photographs and specifications of a new type of bomb being produced in the United States. He claimed that he had photographed it at a plant in Wilmington, Delaware, and since he could not use a light, it had been necessary to expose the film for eight hours. Yet the picture showed a lighted goose-neck lamp! He loved the spectacular, and a little discrepancy like that could hardly throw the effervescent Duquesne.

Next on Sawyer's list of contacts was Lilly Stein. Sawyer wrote her the sort of innocuous yet meaningful letter he had written Duquesne, and immediately received an invitation to meet her in her apartment. Smartly dressed and of better than average appearance, Lilly Stein had enjoyed a varied career up to the moment when Sawyer entered her life. She was born in Vienna of Jewish parents, just after the start of the first World War. Her father had been wealthy enough to provide her with life's luxuries; she had become interested in ice skating, and by frequenting the winter carnivals at the European resorts, she was acquainted with that aspect of international society.

Somewhere in her travels from the Bavarian Alps to Switzerland, she met Heinrich Sorau (or Dr. Hugo Sebold of Hamburg, if you prefer to remember him as such). They became good friends, and he was to prove useful to her because the shadow of Nazi domination was beginning to darken her native country. After the *anschluss* she found herself in serious difficulties; both her parents were dead, and since she was Jewish, she was threatened with the loss of everything she had.

Her good friend Sorau came to the rescue. If she would only work for his "organization" she would be well taken care of. Lilly agreed, and was enrolled in the German espionage service. Her first assignments were in Britain and Belgium, where she helped pave the way for the heavy tread of Nazi boots. She returned to Hamburg for further training in microphotography and coded messages and then left for the United States, which she reached in 1939 by way of Sweden. In the following year, she filed a declaration of intention to become an American citizen, but her arrest as a spy put an end to this laudable idea.

Lilly Stein was one of the three individuals designated to receive the microphotographic instructions. When Sawyer handed her the tiny piece of film, about an inch square, she took a magnifying glass from a drawer and commented merely that she could read it perfectly. By this time Lilly had fallen on evil days. Her hopes of establishing herself in New York society circles had waned;

a women's accessory shop she had opened had failed; her social contacts had fallen off and she was desperately in need of money. Sawyer's arrival filled her with new hope. She met him frequently and turned over to him for transmission to Germany the material she acquired or received, since she operated as a forwarding address for fellow spies in the United States. But her persistent requests for more funds from her German masters, which Sawyer transmitted over the FBI radio, ultimately resulted in instructions from Hamburg for Sawyer to cease working with her.

Like Duquesne, Lilly was put under twenty-four-hour surveillance. All callers were either identified or followed, and all conversations in her apartment were recorded. One of her close friends was Else Weustenfeld, employed in the law office that represented the German Consulate in New York, and also a member of the spy organization. Else's job was to transmit funds and information between Germany and the agents working in this country.

Third on Sawyer's list of instructions was Everett Roeder. An American citizen, he had a comparatively distinguished reputation as draftsman and designer in connection with the manufacture of confidential mechanisms used by the U.S. Army and Navy. An inventor, he derived considerable income from inventions relating to firearms. He visited Germany in 1936, at which time he was approached by the authorities to act as espionage agent for them in the United States. Attracted by the possible remuneration, he agreed to do so.

Sawyer delivered to Roeder his microphotographic memorandum of information sought by the Nazis. Their meetings were always surreptitious. They would meet at railroad stations and other public places, and then would proceed to spots where they could talk in confidence and unmolested. Roeder was probably the greatest producer of detailed technical data on national defense materials and production. At the time Sawyer met him, he was in the employ of the Sperry Gyroscope Company, Inc., a producer of much confidential material for the armed forces. He delivered a wiring diagram of the Lockheed Hudson bomber, diagrams of the plane's gun mounting, and promised to develop new bomb-sight material. But Roeder was a lone operator; he had no relations with the stream of low-life characters who were shortly to make their appearance like flies in Sawyer's parlor.

The last designated agent to whom Sawyer's instructions made

208

reference was Herman Lang. It was noteworthy that no microphotograph of wanted information was made out for this man. The Germans thought far too highly of Lang to cast any suspicion upon him. Why? Because Lang was an employee of Carl L. Norden, Inc., the manufacturer of the famous bomb sight. He was a native of Germany and had come to the United States in 1927. He had been employed by Norden since 1929, and in 1938 he returned to Germany, ostensibly for a brief visit home. In the course of that visit he had conferred with German military authorities in Berlin and had given them from memory the plans of the Norden bomb sight.

By the time Sawyer reached Lang, the spy had become so apprehensive of discovery, because of his close connection with high German authorities and his betrayal of the United States, that his main concern was to get back to Germany. Through Sawyer's radio, arrangements were made for him to go home via Mexico, funds were placed at his disposal and deposits were placed to his credit in German banks. But he hesitated to leave for fear that his departure might create suspicion. As a result, he was taken into custody with the other members of the ring when the trap was sprung.

Sawyer's first assigned tasks were now complete. He had established himself in New York, he had met the key men of the spy ring, he had put into operation a short-wave radio as instructed—although the fact that the FBI was operating it for him was a detail that he did not mention to his Nazi masters. Now he sat back in his office and let the word get around that a new spy boss had arrived who would pay off for information. Meanwhile he cross-examined Duquesne and Lilly Stein, ferreting out the names of their allies so that as many as possible would be taken in the FBI net. Soon the tawdry assortment of German-born spies came streaming into the 42nd Street office—ships' cooks, seamen, stewards, waiters, mechanics—all bringing their trickle of information on ship movements, cargoes, destinations, convoy rendezvous, military and naval data, national defense production. One man led to another. The trail ran from 42nd Street up to the Yorkville section, where Richard Eichenlaub's Little Casino was a hangout for the Hitler-heiling enemies of America. Some were small fry, impelled to work for the German Reich through patriotic zeal for the fatherland, or because they expected rewards, or because they were violently anti-British, under obligation to the Nazis for release from prison, or under threat of reprisals if they failed to carry out instructions.

209

Still others were well-trained professional spies, such as **Paul Fehse**, ostensibly a ship's cook. He was one of the leaders of the agents with whom Sawyer worked. He arranged meetings between them, directed their activities, arranged for reimbursement and generally correlated information and planned for its transmission to Germany, either through Sawyer's radio station or by courier aboard ship or transatlantic clipper. He claimed to be the head of the Marine Division of the German espionage system in the U.S.; like Sawyer, he had been trained in the pension in the Klopstockstrasse.

In all, Sawyer reached 33 German spies. The FBI, of course, could have apprehended any of them at any moment, since they were under constant surveillance, but the plan was to wait as long as possible, let them go as far as they pleased so that all the members of the ring could be implicated. Meanwhile, the information they were attempting to send to Germany was being doctored before its transmittal by radio; their communications to letter drops in various neutral countries were being intercepted by the Allied censorship and turned over to the FBI. Thus, though they were working hard to produce essential information for the fatherland, they were in reality of no service once they came under the Bureau's eyes.

At last, during the weekend of June 28, 1941, the trap was sprung. Thirty-three members of the ring were arrested in New York City and other places. They were indicted on charges of violating espionage statutes as well as failing to register as agents of foreign principals. Nineteen of them pleaded guilty when the FBI showed its hand; the other 14 pleaded not guilty. Their trial began in the Federal District Court on September 3. Hundreds of candid photographs and thousands of feet of motion picture film of the various spies conferring with Sawyer in his office were shown at the trial. Sawyer, of course, was the chief witness, and Special Agents who had installed the recording apparatus, built the radio and kept close surveillance on the suspects appeared to build up a fool-proof case against them. On December 13, more than three months later, all were found guilty by a jury of nine men and three women, although one of the accused later succeeded in an appeal. They were sentenced in January to more than 320 years in prison, and were fined a total of $18,000.

So ended the career of the biggest spy ring ever to operate in the United States. There were other spies, of course; they kept coming over from Germany with almost automatic regularity. By 1940, the normal channels for enemy agents to enter the U.S. had been closed. The Nazis then resorted to the device of sending spies over in the guise of refugees—persons who, under pressure, had agreed to work for Germany. The joker was that the FBI knew all about them, expected their arrival, and were on hand with a welcoming party when the "refugee from Nazi terror" stepped down the gangplank. The strategy of the FBI was then to lay its cards on the table, tell the spy it knew all about him, and give him the alternative of working with the FBI or being apprehended. Most of them chose to work with the Bureau. These "double agents," as they were called, had to be kept under close surveillance, of course, lest they betray both Hitler and America, but they were extremely valuable in leading the FBI to other spies.

Among such "double agents" was Grace Buchanan-Dineen, who arrived in this country with an immense wardrobe, ready to spy for Hitler. The fact that she cooperated with the FBI did not prevent the judge who heard her case from giving her a prison sentence, but it lightened her term. Another famous "refugee" was Dieudonne Costes, the French aviator who flew from Paris to New York in 1930. Under pressure, he had joined the German Intelligence Service in 1942, was trained in espionage procedure and left France in the same year. A month later he made connections with an American source in Spain. As a result, when Paul Cavaillez, a Frenchman who had served in the French Air Force, turned up in the United States and set about buying radio parts and installing a receiver near Locust Valley, Long Island, he was placed under arrest. Cavaillez was the man with whom Costes had been instructed to team up.

While the Duquesne ring was still in operation, the FBI's attention was drawn to a curious letter intercepted by the British censorship at Bermuda. This was in January, 1941, and by the end of the same year, nine more German spies were under arrest. It was not so simple as it sounds. This case, known as the Ludwig case, took a lot of cracking.

The letter turned over to the FBI was apparently innocuous in content. It was signed simply "Joe K" and was written to an address in Spain. Examination of the letter in the FBI Laboratory, however, revealed that on the back there was detailed information regarding the identities and cargoes of ships sailing from New York

211

for Great Britain. This was written in invisible ink. That was all the FBI had to go on. Then the British censorship turned up subsequent letters addressed to persons in Spain, Portugal, Germany and Argentina, all signed "Joe K" or "J.K." Like the first, they carried secret information, and their return addresses were found to be fictitious.

Who, among all New York's millions, was "Joe K"? That was the problem the FBI faced. Here fate lent a hand. On the evening of March 18 there was an accident in Times Square. Two men were walking east across the square at 45th Street about 11 o'clock. One of them, paying no attention to the traffic lights, stepped in front of a taxi and was hurled into the path of another oncoming car. He was a tall, middle-aged man carrying a brown brief case. His companion, after making a futile gesture to restrain his friend, swiftly grabbed up the brief case and disappeared into the crowd.

The fatally injured man was taken to a hospital, where it was found that he was Julio Lopez Lido. In his pockets were about $64 and numerous papers, most of them in German. In a small notebook there was mention of a powder plant and the names and places of assignment of several United States Army officers. The man was registered at a hotel in the vicinity of Times Square, and when the local police searched his room, they concluded rightly that the FBI would be interested in the case.

An unidentified caller telephoned the hotel and asked that the injured man's room be held until further notice. He said he was a friend, and refused to give his name. After Lido's death in the hospital, his body lay unclaimed for a time until burial arrangements were made and paid for by the Spanish Consulate. The funeral was shrouded in mystery. Labels had been removed from the dead man's clothing, and only four women were present at the funeral. They declined to give their names and addresses and refused the undertaker's offer to drive them to their respective homes after the service.

All the resources of the FBI were now turned upon this strange case. For in the dead man's room the New York police had found a card issued in 1929 to one Ulrich von der Osten by the American Consulate in Berlin, showing that the subject was a German. They had also found a bottle of a German patent remedy, good for headaches but also excellent for preparing invisible ink.

Who was von der Osten? The FBI soon had the answer. Captain Ulrich von der Osten had arrived in Honolulu via Japan on

212

February 21, 1941, aboard the liner *President Cleveland*. He was carried on the manifest as Julio Lopez Lido and was described as a Spanish national, born in Cadiz. He arrived in the United States on February 27, and attached the following letter to his baggage declaration:

"To Whom It May Concern: The Spanish subject Señor Don Julio Lopez is carrying the official mail bag of this representative of Spain in China to the Consul General of Spain in New York City, U.S.A., for which I request the competent authorities not only to put no obstructions in the journey but to grant him all the facilities and help he may need during same, according to the usual diplomatic concessions granted in such cases."

Von der Osten went immediately to New York City and then left for Colorado to visit a brother. He returned to New York on March 15, only three days before the accident that took his life. He had come to New York to direct the activities of the group of spies of which "Joe K" was a member, for he was one of the chiefs of the German Intelligence Service whose duty it was to do business with individual spies throughout the world. He had visited the United States in 1929 and 1934, although the ship's manifest stated that he had never entered the country before. His career as a spy director in the Second World War was short-lived, but before his death he had written a letter to his principals abroad that illustrated his perspicacity.

"My journeys through the country," he wrote, "have in the meantime shown me that this beautiful country is really in earnest. All the reports about internal political disputes, 'bottlenecks,' etc., do not, in actual fact, mean much. Everything is working to the best possible means . . . much is being achieved. The government has the country entirely behind it. . . ."

So much for von der Osten. He was dead and gone. Who was to take his place in the job that he had vacated so suddenly? The FBI was soon to find out. Among the dead man's effects were names and addresses of his associates. A careful investigation of these names led to Lucy Boehmler, German born, 17 years of age, who lived in a Long Island town. Meanwhile, Agents were investigating every clue, which ultimately led them to the man they had been seeking for months—"Joe K."

Agents identified him as Kurt Frederick Ludwig, an Ohio-born pocketbook maker. He had lived with his parents in the United

213

States until he was about 6 years old, when they took him to live in Germany. He had thereafter divided his time between the two countries, finally returning to America in 1940. Shortly after his return, he was introduced to Lucy Boehmler by Mrs. Helen Mayer, a 26-year-old Queens housewife, who was also a gymnastics instructor in the New York Turnverein and an active German agent. Ludwig became very friendly with Lucy and her family and visited their home frequently. In March, 1941, he informed her about his connections with the German Reich and told her he wanted her to meet Phil Lopez, who was anxious to hire her as his secretary.

Lucy thereupon met Phil Lopez, or von der Osten, and agreed to work for him in full knowledge that he was a member of the German espionage service. She had hardly begun her job when von der Osten was killed.

Now both Lucy and Ludwig were under twenty-four-hour watch. It was apparent to the Agents tailing Ludwig that he had decided to carry on in the dead man's place. He began gathering espionage information with the greatest fervor. He visited the New York waterfront and the docks on the Jersey shore, traveling to and fro on the Weehawken ferry, noting ships and cargoes. He visited Army posts, observing troop strengths, identities of units, the quality and quantity of their arms and equipment, and any details which he believed would aid the fatherland. Specimens from his typewriter and of his handwriting were obtained by the FBI men; the Laboratory soon confirmed his identity as the man who had been sending letters abroad in secret ink. He carried innocent-looking white pills with him. When they were dissolved in a glass of water he had invisible ink, and a few toothpicks in his vest pocket served as a pen that could be instantly discarded. He was an enthusiastic amateur photographer. His favorite subjects appeared to be Army and Navy training posts, power stations, harbors, aircraft, engines, bridges and public utility nerve centers.

He had already written to his foreign superiors to tell them about the Times Square accident. "This week something terrible happened," he wrote. "Phil, whom you know too, had a fatal accident. One evening he wanted to cross Broadway . . ." and so on. The letter, like his others, was intercepted by the British and turned over to the FBI. In his numerous communications abroad Ludwig constantly disguised his meaning by writing what purported to be business letters· "What do you think of the samples I sent you lately?

Do you think you could do any business with them?"

Before von der Osten's death, he and Ludwig had planned an extensive tour of Atlantic Coast defense points and military installations, and then on across the southern states to California. Now Ludwig and Lucy undertook a trip to Florida, driving past Army camps, flying fields and war production centers. It was here that Lucy was useful. She would joke with passing soldiers near the camps and pry information out of them. On one occasion, when they were returning from Florida, they passed a large convoy of trucks in Pennsylvania loaded with soldiers. Ludwig remarked that he would like to know where they had come from and where they were going. So while he drove slowly alongside the trucks, Lucy leaned out of the window and made herself pleasant to the troops. When she stopped flirting, she had the name of the camp the men had left and their destination. Thereupon she located the Pennsylvania camp on the map, while Ludwig counted the trucks and estimated the number of men being transferred.

In Florida, Ludwig got in touch with Carl Schroetter, a Miami boat captain, through whom he was able to report to Germany concerning the progress being made in the construction of naval air base facilities there. Meanwhile, in New York, Helen Mayer was handling his correspondence through his post office box. Back home, Ludwig was seen to meet Rene Froehlich, an enlisted man in the United States Army, stationed at Governors Island in New York harbor. As a soldier, Froehlich had army publications sent to him and these he turned over to Ludwig for transmission to Germany. Thus one by one Ludwig's associates were slowly being enmeshed in the net thrown out by the FBI. Hans Pagel and Frederick Schlosser, two youths of German birth and Nazi ideology, who assisted him in making observations around New York's docks and military installations, soon dropped into the hopper. Karl Mueller, who assisted him in mailing letters to foreign addresses, soon had an FBI man for a constant but unsuspected companion. Major Paul Borchardt, who held lengthy conferences with Ludwig as the technical adviser of the group and had in his possession equipment for writing invisible ink messages, was shortly under surveillance.

Time was drawing short for Ludwig and his companions. He was presently to get a big fright. Two of the spies involved in the Duquesne ring were apprehended in a New York bookstore in June, 1941. Ludwig was present at the time, but the Special Agents making the arrest pretended not to notice him and allowed him to continue his activities. "I missed a serious accident only by inches," he wrote to his superiors. He was neither questioned nor noticed, he said. "What luck amidst bad luck—but I had a fright." When he learned the extent of the arrests, it shook him to his boot leather. He was so upset that he ceased his activities and went off to a summer resort in the Poconos. There he sat on the front lawn, mostly by himself, presumably recovering from the shock.

Early in August he began a furious automobile trip to the West Coast. He drove like a hunted man, forcing his car along the country roads of the Midwest as fast as 90 miles an hour. The Special Agents following him had quite a job to keep up with him. He stopped long enough en route at strategic points to make notes of what he saw. At Wright Field, Ohio, he stopped to change a flat tire; the Agents saw him closely observing the activities at the field as he worked. Near Indianapolis he put his car in a parking lot and on foot watched the traffic going by. Then he got in his car again, drove to another parking lot and repeated the process. Near Selfridge Field, Michigan, he picked up two soldiers and began asking them harmless questions. Could the planes lined up on the field be bought for around $1,200? he asked. The men laughed and told him they were worth $30,000 apiece. Then he wanted to know if they could fly at about the speed of a car. There was a large cement mixer along the road and he asked whether this was an antiaircraft gun.

By the time he reached Yellowstone National Park, Ludwig appeared to be in a nervous state. He spent a night in a tourist cabin where he burned papers taken from his car, and it became obvious that he was preparing to leave the country and return to Germany by way of the Orient. He was not successful, by the way, in destroying all the incriminating evidence in his possession. From Yellowstone he continued to Butte, Montana, where he shipped his personal belongings to relatives in New Jersey. He stored his car in Missoula because, as he admitted later, he was too jittery to drive farther. It contained an expensive short-wave radio receiver.

Then he went on by bus to Cle Elum, near Seattle, where, on August 23, Special Agents took him into custody. Eight of his associates were picked up in the East. For months the nine had been kept under constant surveillance; every move had been recorded. The FBI had scored its second smashing blow against German agents in America. Lucy Boehmler, who became a Government witness, was sentenced to five years' imprisonment. The other eight received sentences ranging from 10 to 20 years.

As in the Duquesne case, the FBI had allowed the spies to operate as long as possible before making arrests. For in tracking down spies an entirely different strategy must be employed from that used in apprehending bank robbers or kidnapers. It would be simple to arrest a spy the moment he is identified. It would also be extremely convenient for the foreign government concerned: it would simply assign another man to fill the place of the convicted spy, and the FBI would be back at the starting point once more. The FBI believes that the real test of its effectiveness lies in the number of spies located, contacts established and sources of information uncovered and controlled. The underlings of espionage are relatively harmless and their arrest accomplishes little. But when placed under surveillance, even the smallest fry may lead to bigger fish.

That was what happened in the cases related above. These were the most spectacular of the spy rings operating in this country, but there were other spies and traitors being investigated while the United States was still at peace.

Peace was a commodity that was growing scarce in the world. The Bureau worked with frantic haste to glean all possible information on potential enemies. Data was accumulated regarding those visitors to America whose loyalty was still with the fatherland, those who would be dangerous should war come, those who would make up Hitler's fifth column in the United States. By December 1, 1941, these plans called for the immediate arrest of several thousand Germans, Italians and Japanese, all of whom were under constant scrutiny, if war came.

As it had come to so many countries of the Old World, war came at last to the United States with a furious suddenness that left the nation momentarily reeling. The Japanese bombs that smashed at Pearl Harbor set into action the FBI's war plans, developed through the years of Nazi aggression. While the attack on Pearl Harbor was still in progress, the Special Agent in Charge of the Honolulu office was in touch with Washington headquarters. Every Field Office from Alaska to Puerto Rico was alerted. Every FBI employee in each office was at his assigned post of duty within the hour. The Bureau was put on a twenty-four-hour basis; all annual leave was cancelled. The FBI moved at unprecedented

217

speed to prevent sabotage. All dangerous Japanese who had been under scrutiny were picked up. Air lines were ordered to refuse transportation to any Japanese or to accept shipments from Japanese nationals. Japs aboard planes crossing the country were removed. Telephone communication to and from enemy countries was suspended. Press services to Japan and occupied China were cut off. Guards were thrown around the German, Japanese and Italian Embassies in Washington, and at such Japanese Consulates as were still open throughout the country; mail and telephone services were discontinued and their funds were frozen.

The communications section of the Bureau, with its 20,000 miles of teletype circuits, became more than ever the nerve center of the widely separated Field Offices. Within the first 36 hours after the initial bombs fell on Pearl Harbor, 19 teletype conferences with all the continental offices were held. So urgent were many of these messages that they were dictated directly to the teletype operators instead of to stenographers. Special Agents in Charge were instructed to take into custody all Japanese whose names appeared on lists the FBI already had prepared. All Japanese aliens who might prove dangerous were also apprehended and turned over to the Immigration and Naturalization officers.

On the following day, all German and Italian aliens in certain categories were rounded up. By December 9, the Attorney General was able to announce that by the previous evening 1,771 alien enemies had been apprehended with the cooperation of local law enforcement officers.

It was only natural, with the country so suddenly precipitated into war, that a certain amount of public hysteria should manifest itself. Wild rumors circulated in Hawaii, to reappear later on the mainland. Immediate investigation of such rumors of spies and sabotage did much to restore jittery nerves, and the orderly apprehension of dangerous aliens restored the confidence of loyal and patriotic aliens that they had nothing to fear at the hands of the Bureau. Vigilante organizations were discouraged; the witch-hunting and mass raids of the first World War were absent, and the fear of an American fifth column subsided as quickly as it had sprung up.

Confidence in the internal security of the country was restored to an amazing extent when the 33 members of the Duquesne spy ring were convicted in the first week after Pearl Harbor. The trial and conviction of the Ludwig gang further staggered German Intelligence and bolstered American confidence. In all, the FBI, with the aid of local officers, rounded up more than 16,000 alien enemies; by December 1, 1944, some 4,000 were interned for the duration, nearly 6,000 were placed under restrictive parole, 3,000 were released without hearings, and about 2,000 were released after explaining their actions or were repatriated to their native countries.

The residences of many aliens were searched for contraband material. The FBI checked more than 25,000 enemy premises and, despite warnings to aliens to turn such items in, they seized 4,626 firearms, 2,240 sticks of dynamite, 3,127 short-wave radio receivers, 4,245 cameras, hundreds of thousands of rounds of ammunition, thousands of swords, daggers, dirks and blasting caps, and quantities of maps, charts and code books. These individuals, who might have formed a dangerous fifth column when the nation was militarily weak and unprepared, were stripped of their weapons and were brought before hearing boards.

Meanwhile the Bureau pressed its investigations against suspected enemy agents, saboteurs and disloyal citizens. As we have seen, the normal channels for enemy agents to enter the country were closed in 1940. The German Intelligence thereupon applied to Admiral Doenitz for the use of U-boats to transport saboteurs to the United States. The admiral agreed, with the proviso that such information as these saboteurs could transmit to the fatherland be made available to the German Navy, and to the submarine branch in particular.

In the prewar years and after Pearl Harbor the FBI had enrolled loyal and patriotic citizens as watchmen on the home front. By early 1942 there were more than 6,000 of these confidential national defense informants. Many of them were in coastal areas, where they were ready to alert the FBI to anything of a suspicious nature. Many reports of suspected landings of enemy agents from submarines were checked without result.

On June 13, 1942, the FBI received the information they had been expecting. Suspicious persons had been seen on the beach at Amagansett, Long Island. A Coast Guardsman had challenged individuals and had turned in an alarm; equipment found on the beach was handed over to the FBI. But several hours had elapsed between the landing and the report to the FBI. The invaders had made their way to New York, there to lose themselves among the millions crowded into the vast metropolitan area.

Director Hoover mobilized the Bureau's entire facilities for the most extensive manhunt it had ever conducted.

On the following evening, the New York office of the FBI received information that a person who gave his name as Franz Daniel Pastorius was possibly involved in this case. The Bureau redoubled its vigilance; it checked a reported landing in Massachusetts; in Florida an unlighted seaplane landed offshore at night; a Special Agent flying over the Gulf Coast spotted oil drums at a secluded point. The FBI knew that the sabotage attempts were long overdue, but it did not know how many submarines might be en route with saboteurs. At a conference in Florida, local law enforcement officers were informed that the Germans had already attempted to land in the United States, and they were warned to be on the lookout for further landings.

FBI Agents throughout the entire United States were on the alert in the hope that some clue would be found to the identity of the mysterious Franz Daniel Pastorius. When would a break come in the case? On Friday morning, June 19, a man later identified as George John Dasch, one of the saboteurs, was located by two Special Agents in a Washington hotel. Dasch, it was learned, was identical with Franz Daniel Pastorius. Escorted to FBI Headquarters, Dasch told of his sabotage mission and said his group had landed on Long Island from a submarine. From Dasch, Agents obtained information that led to the location of another saboteur, Ernest Peter Burger, in New York. He was placed under close surveillance.

Dasch then related that another group of four saboteurs had been ordered to land near Jacksonville, Florida, under the command of one Edward Kerling. He could not recall the names of the men who had landed with him at Amagansett, but he knew their aliases. Of the Florida group he could remember only that one was a young man from Chicago, another used the alias Nicholas and the third had assumed the *nom de guerre* of John Thomas. It was here that the files which the FBI had painstakingly built up in the prewar years came to the rescue. Dasch could not identify his companions, but the FBI had a very good idea who they might be. The Agent interviewing Dasch was able, by consulting the records of known Nazi sympathizers, to identify the Chicago man as Herbert Hans Haupt. A further check of the records disclosed that Kerling, while in the United States, had been friendly with Hermann Otto Neubauer.

220

Neubauer's record and photographs were shown to Dasch. He immediately identified Neubauer as the person he knew as Nicholas.

Then Dasch recalled that the aliases used by the saboteurs began with the first two letters of their real names. The Agent therefore opened a Washington telephone directory, turned the pages until he came to names beginning with "Th," and began to read down the column. When he came to the name Thiel, Dasch halted him. "That's it," he said. "Werner Thiel."

Further reference to Kerling's file produced information about his wife and other close allies in the New York area. They were placed under surveillance. From Dasch the Agents took a pocket handkerchief. In the Laboratory it was found to bear in invisible ink the names of several persons who were to act as aides for the saboteurs. They were located and placed under surveillance.

On June 20, the close watch maintained on saboteurs and their confederates began to produce results. Burger left his hotel in the afternoon and proceeded to a men's furnishings store at Fifth Avenue and 41st Street. Later he met two men wearing new clothes and corresponding to the description of the other two saboteurs given by Dasch. After conferring for some time, the three separated. Burger's two companions, Heinrich Heinck and Richard Quirin, were followed to the vicinity of 75th Street and Amsterdam Avenue, where they were quietly arrested. Burger was trailed back to his hotel, where he was also put under arrest. Thus the Long Island group of saboteurs was cleaned up, but the Florida gang was still at large.

Meanwhile, Haupt's home in Chicago was under surveillance. His friends were watched. On June 22, Haupt himself walked into the Chicago office of the FBI. He was given a routine interview by a Special Agent, who was aware of his identity. Haupt told the Agent that he had learned the FBI had called at his home several months before with reference to his Selective Service status. He explained that he had been in Mexico all the time, because of a love affair with a girl he did not wish to marry. He gave his home address, said he had straightened himself out with his local draft board, and asked if it would be all right for him to go back to work.

The Agent told him with a straight face that the FBI had no further interest in his draft status since he had cleared it up. Haupt then left the office, apparently confident that he had outwitted the FBI and thrown it off guard. He was unaware that he was under constant surveillance, or that he was being allowed his liberty merely to lead the FBI to his companions.

The following day in New York there were further developments in this swiftly moving drama. One of the men whose name had appeared on Dasch's handkerchief was followed to a spot near Pennsylvania Station, where he met a person answering Kerling's description. The stranger was followed immediately. That evening he met two men in a 44th Street bar; one of them answered to Thiel's description. The men separated. Kerling was followed to Lexington Avenue between 49th and 50th Streets, where he was picked up. Thiel was followed to 42nd Street and taken into custody.

When Kerling finally agreed to talk, he admitted that his party had landed south of Jacksonville Beach early in the morning of June 17 and had buried their explosives and equipment. The cache was found to be identical with that buried on the Long Island beach. By this time the FBI had recovered a large sum from the saboteurs. Dasch had $82,550 and Kerling had $3,800 in a money belt. In the hotel room occupied by him and Thiel $54,550 was found. Recoveries from the other saboteurs eventually raised the amount to $174,588.62, which was turned over to the United States Treasury.

In Chicago the surveillance of Haupt continued, but his companion Neubauer had not yet been located. The minute check continued until finally, on June 27, Agents found that an "H. Nicholas" had registered at a hotel. When Nicholas appeared he was identified as Neubauer and was arrested; simultaneously Haupt was apprehended. Thus, within 14 days after their arrival in the United States, all eight saboteurs were in custody.

Officials of plants and facilities on the list for attack were advised by telephone to be on guard for future sabotage attempts. The list included the TVA Project, source of power for the atomic bomb project; plants of the Aluminum Company of America; the Cryolite plant at Philadelphia; the Chesapeake and Ohio Railroad; the Pennsylvania Railroad depot at Newark, New Jersey; the Hell Gate Bridge in New York City; Ohio River Locks between Cincinnati and St. Louis; and the horseshoe curve of the Pennsylvania Railroad at Altoona, Pennsylvania. Panic and terror were also to be caused by placing time bombs in railroad lockers and in crowded department stores.

All eight men were tried before a military commission. All were sentenced to death, but Dasch and Burger received Presidential clemency upon the recommendation of Director Hoover, with the concurrence of the Attorney General. Both were sent to Federal prisons, Dasch serving a 30-year sentence and Burger a life term.

Thus the FBI faced and met its greatest challenge. The colossal failure of the first attempts to land saboteurs in America caused a change in German plans. It had been intended that every six weeks a group would debark from Nazi submarines off the coast of the United States and proceed to wreak havoc in the nation. Only two more were dispatched. They landed in Maine in November, 1944, and like their predecessors, they ran into the outstretched arms of the FBI soon after their arrival. The German High Command had reckoned without the FBI.

There is an epilogue to the story of Germany's espionage in the United States. It was written by the Nazis themselves—by the Reich Foreign Office and the German High Command. Six years after the Duquesne spy ring had been smashed and its members convicted, an echo of the case stirred faintly amid the wreckage of Berlin. Hitler's Chancellery lay in ruins, his Reich that was to last 1,000 years was smashed, and the war crimes trials at Nürnberg were drawing to a close. In the last days of August, 1946, the FBI came into possession of certain documents from the German Foreign Office files relating to spy and saboteur activities in America. They are published here for the first time.

They show that the German Embassy in Washington was at loggerheads with Abwehr, the arm of the High Command to which espionage and counterintelligence were entrusted. The Embassy feared that such Nazi activity in the United States would embroil that country in war with Germany while the Embassy's task was to keep America neutral at all costs. Actually, the Embassy had not been consulted and was piqued. The Embassy had no high opinion of the men entrusted by the Army to carry out such tasks. Admiral Canaris, the head of the German Intelligence Services, on the other hand, felt that the military information developed by these agents was highly valuable to Germany, and he pointedly told the Embassy to mind its own affairs.

It was as early as May, 1940, that Dr. Hans Thomsen, Charge d'Affaires of the German Embassy, cabled the Foreign Office in

Berlin regarding his apprehensions.

"I have been under the impression," he wrote, "that the activity of the agents of the army under orders in the U.S. would commence only in a crisis, that is, after severance of relations or declaration of war. The fact that this is not the case can be seen from a statement of an agent who, tormented by doubts concerning the necessity of his actions, advised an official of the Consulate General in New York that he had received orders from Major Osten to organize sabotage in U.S.A. . . . He alleges to have been convinced that just the opposite would be attained by carrying out the orders given him as was intended, especially since the subagents assigned to him were mostly useless braggarts. . . . I am not able to review the extent of the net of agents; however, it appears . . . to be a matter of systematized organization. If it is my chief task to prevent with all available means the entrance of the U.S. into the war and to cultivate the few valuable relationships which we still have here, such tasks will be sabotaged outright by the above-mentioned activity of the agents of the army."

The Wilhelmstrasse hastened to assure Dr. Thomsen that his mission in the United States was not endangered. Baron Ernst von Weizsäcker, at that time Under Secretary in the Foreign Office, replied that military offices had expressly stated that there were no orders issued to commit sabotage of any kind in or against America.

But after the arrest of the Duquesne ring, the Charge d'Affaires in Washington let go another blast at the High Command. Again he had not been consulted and was calling attention to his grievance against the Abwehr. On July 7, 1941, he cabled the Foreign Office in part as follows:

"Most and apparently all of the people involved in this affair were . . . completely unadapted for such activity. In order to make themselves appear important these people continually pointed out in their groups that they were under such orders and were carrying them out. It is to be assumed that the American authorities knew of the entire network, which certainly was no work of art in view of the naive and to a certain extent downright stupid manner in the way these people carried on."

It is obvious that by this time Thomsen had needled the Foreign Office into taking up with Abwehr the question of the 33 spies whose arrest in New York had created such an unfavorable atmosphere for the successful continuation of the Washington mission.

In a detailed report to the Foreign Office, Abwehr replied to Thomsen's charges on July 23, 1941. It listed the information produced by the men who had worked for the organization in the United States, and in a bristling concluding passage, Admiral Canaris virtually told Dr. Thomsen that he didn't know what he was talking about, and demanded that his charges against the Abwehr be withdrawn.

What did the Nazi High Command think of the men it had hired to spy in the United States? On the whole, it thought pretty highly of them and their achievements. Of Everett Roeder it reported: "He has been active for Abwehr since 1937. He has delivered valuable technical material in the original, including remote control machine-gun sight, bombsight, blind flight instruments, bank indicator, course indicator, speech scrambler, radio equipment on airplanes for Russia. Most items delivered were designated as 'valuable,' some as 'very valuable' and 'of great importance.' "

Duquesne had also "delivered valuable reports and important technical material in the original, including U.S. gas masks, radio control apparatus, leakproof fuel tanks, television instruments, small bombs for airplanes versus airplanes, air separator and propeller driving mechanism. Items delivered were labeled 'valuable,' and several 'good' and 'very good.' "

Herman Lang was very highly thought of indeed by the German General Staff. He had "delivered technical material in the original, important and decisive in the prosecution of the war. In a statement by the Office of Air Force Equipment it is stated: 'As a result of delivery by this agent of technical sketches and elements of construction of a bombsight accompanied by explanatory remarks, it was possible to reconstruct the implement. The device promises ample interesting technical solutions, constructively shows good development and constitutes the climax to a period of detailed research. The marksmanships attained in U.S. are extraordinarily good. Such efficiency has not as yet been attained in Germany. Considerable research expenses have been saved by the delivery of these items. In actual tests of the device it was revealed that the principle realized therein reacted favorably for the projected bomb drop. Accordingly, the items concerning the bombsight delivered from the U.S.A. by the Abwehr have successfully influenced the development of the German bombsights.'

"The special importance of the deliveries by this agent can

225

be seen from the fact that the American bombsights are far superior to those of other powers, as a result of which great secrecy is maintained concerning them; also the pilots are instructed to destroy the bombsight in case the airplanes must land in enemy territory."

Admiral Canaris then concluded his report with the following thrust aimed at Dr. Thomsen:

"The success of the secret military intelligence service which is confirmed again and again by our military offices sufficiently proves that the structure of the intelligence network or the selection of agents in and for U.S.A. have been necessary and correct."

It is apparent from the documents that the arrest of the Duquesne ring and publication of the part played by Harry Sawyer threw German military and Foreign Office circles into something of a panic. "Representatives of interested offices in Germany met together in reference thereto, at which time it was apparent certain justifications were called for," a memorandum dated September 18, 1941, in Berlin reveals. At this conference it was stated that Sawyer "has been an agent of the Hamburg Abwehr office. Until very recently there was no suspicion concerning him. The only thing of notice was the fact that although radio contact still existed no or very little and unessential material was delivered." Thus the Germans admitted that Sawyer had completely fooled them.

A further memorandum again bearing this out, dated in Berlin October 1, 1941, is translated in part as follows:

"On the basis of confidential communications from the OKW (Supreme Command of the Armed Forces) and knowledge from the files, I have the following picture: Sawyer was an agent of the Abwehr office in Hamburg, which until very recently had no doubts concerning his reliability. Due to the fact that he had radio contact with Hamburg, numerous orders to our other agents went via him, so it was very easy for him to turn over information on all Abwehr agents in U.S.A. to his real employer, the FBI. The false documents and misleading data placed in the hands of a few agents had been designated in an earlier letter from Abwehr as valuable reports, most all of which were rated as 'of extreme interest' by the interested offices."

It was Admiral Canaris of Abwehr headquarters who had the last word regarding the espionage trials in New York. In a letter dated Berlin, October 11, 1941, to the Foreign Office, he insisted, as before, that the information that had been developed was highly valuable. He declared that suspicion of Harry Sawyer's role was aroused shortly after the double agent began his work in New York, a contention that is hard to believe when the extent and duration of Sawyer's radio contact with Hamburg and his dealings with the other members of the ring are recalled. Canaris took a final crack at the Foreign Office, saying that German agents working in the United States got no help from either the Embassy or the consulates.

In connection with the Sawyer espionage case, the following alibi was prepared for the record in an attempt to save face:

"In February, 1939, Sawyer returned to Germany from U.S.A. and was directed via the Düsseldorf Gestapo and the Münster Abwehr office to the Hamburg Abwehr office. In February, 1940, he was sent to the U.S.A. A short time after he had assumed his activity in U.S.A. the suspicion was aroused at Abwehr that his reports, although some of them were rated as very favorable by Air Force Headquarters and no unfavorable comments were made concerning them by the Naval High Command, were to be accepted with caution. Thus, for example, a report concerning certain plans of the Air Force in U.S.A. were recognized here as worthless. Some of the reports were even filed without any further action.

"The suspicion of Abwehr which soon extended also to the reliability of Sawyer himself was confirmed by the fact that this agent requested the code of another transmitter (Max) for which he was used merely as a relay station. In spite of several requests he was not given this code. Then in forwarding orders to the Max transmitter Sawyer forged the ciphers. That, too, was soon discovered and strengthened the mistrust concerning Sawyer. Shortly thereafter the relay station was given up. . . .

"It must be stated that the (Abwehr) agents working in U.S.A. were compelled to carry out their work without any support from the German Embassy and the German consulates as long as they were in U.S.A. Neither financial support nor the use of diplomatic couriers for transmittal of information could be used since the Embassy and consulates strictly refused any cooperation.

Chief of the Supreme Command of the Armed Forces
per Canaris."

The Nazis in the U.S. had grown bold when this huge meeting of the Bund was held in Madison Square Garden, New York, in 1939.
228

In every United States city with a large German community, scenes like this were an everyday commonplace. Here three members of the German-American Bund give the Nazi salute to a portrait of Hitler in the New York headquarters of their organization. One of these men, Helmuth Leiner (center), was later taken into custody by the FBI because of assistance he gave a German saboteur.

But the FBI had its eye on the instigators. Telephoto movie cameras were installed opposite the German Embassy in Washington, and

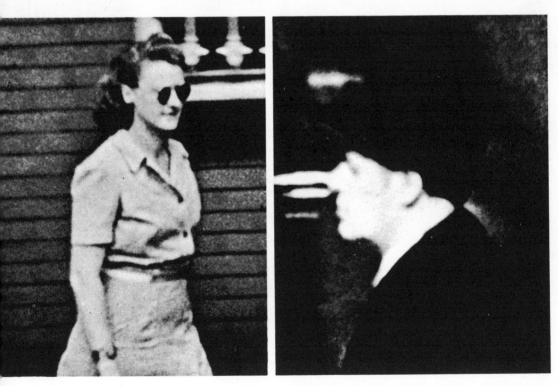

callers were kept under surveillance. It was soon determined that the Embassy was at least a focal point for spy activities.

Homes of alien enemies searched by the FBI revealed prohibited materials in great quantity, in violation of Presidential proclamations. Cameras, radios and parts, binoculars, pistols, revolvers and automatic weapons were turned up by the thousands.

Saboteurs began their deadly work. In 1942 a Southern Pacific railroad bridge in California was destroyed by fire. The arsonist, later convicted on FBI evidence, was an avowed hater of the U.S. Government, but had no connection with the nation's wartime enemies. Not a single case of enemy-directed sabotage was uncovered in the U.S. in the second World War.

When Kurt Ludwig was arrested, this picture of the entrance to the Cuyahoga River from Lake Erie was found in his camera.

On his fast trips around the country he made pictures such as this and rushed them to Germany by courier on ships and air clippers.

233

This is the office Harry Sawyer leased in New York at the direction of the FBI. He occupied the chair at the desk; his visitors sat at the right, facing the mirror on the wall through which the Agents in the next office took moving pictures and made records.

From the other side of the "X-ray" mirror Sawyer's office appeared like this. The spies were caught full-face by the camera as they handed over information and received payment. Here, in *The House on 92nd Street,* Leo G. Carroll enacts the role of Duquesne.

235

In earlier days Duquesne was resplendent as a German officer (top left); when the FBI photographed him in 1940, his appearance had altered considerably. With him (bottom left) is Harry Sawyer.

Some spies in the Duquesne ring as seen through the "X-ray" mirror: Paul Fehse and Leo Waalen (top), Franz Stigler (center) and Erwin Siegler (bottom) enthusiastically turn over their information.

The Nazis evolved a brilliant method of transmitting secret information by reducing a printed page some 250 times to pinhead size. The instrument they used to prepare these microdots is shown here.

The tiny dot of film was then fastened into a punctuation mark in a letter, or to the dotted pattern of an envelope as shown above.

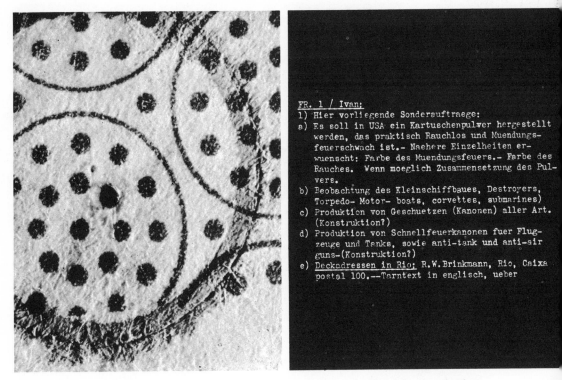

FR. 1 / Ivan:
1) Hier vorliegende Sonderauftraege:
a) Es soll in USA ein Kartuschenpulver hergestellt
   werden, das praktisch Rauchlos und Muendungs-
   feuerschwach ist.- Naehere Einzelheiten er-
   wuenscht: Farbe des Muendungsfeuers.- Farbe des
   Rauches. Wenn moeglich Zusammensetzung des Pul-
   vers.
b) Beobachtung des Kleinschiffbaues, Destroyers,
   Torpedo- Motor- boats, corvettes, submarines)
c) Produktion von Geschuetzen (Kanonen) aller Art.
   (Konstruktion?)
d) Produktion von Schnellfeuerkanonen fuer Flug-
   zeuge und Tanks, sowie anti-tank und anti-air
   guns-(Konstruktion?)
e) Deckadressen in Rio: R.W.Brinkmann, Rio, Caixa
   postal 100.--Tarntext in englisch, ueber

Here the microdot can be seen in the center of the black circle. When it is enlarged, a page of printed matter or plans is visible.

239

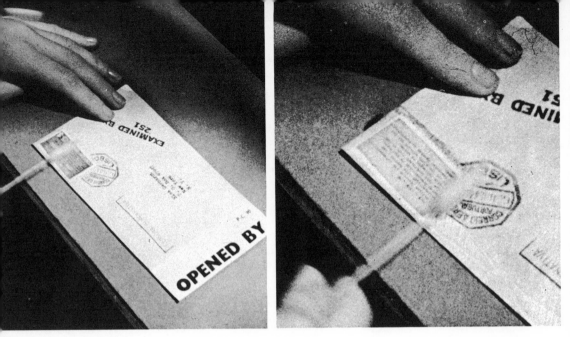

The Nazis communicated with their agents in the U.S. by placing
the message on a stamp. It was made visible by a chemical reagent.

One Nazi agent attempted to smuggle in microphotographs of instructions concealed in a wax disc embedded in a jar of cold cream.

240

Duquesne used a rubber stamp of a cat as a seal on his letters. The
ring conveyed information by notes hidden in cigarette packs.

Joseph Klein, one of the Duquesne spy ring members, built a radio
and had a friend take this incriminating picture found by the FBI.

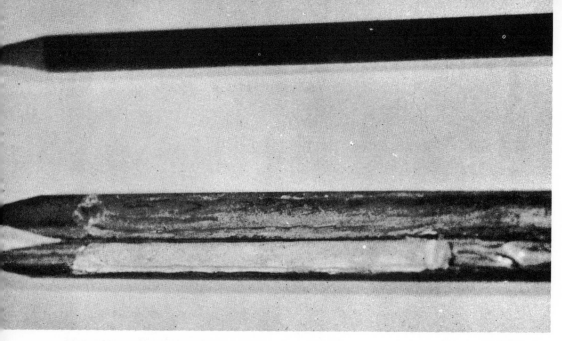

The German saboteurs brought several ingenious devices. This picture shows how an incendiary mechanism was concealed in a pencil.

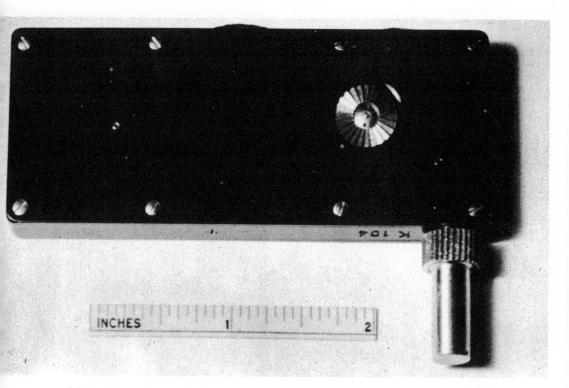

This tiny time clock, made with jeweler's precision, could be set to detonate explosive charges minutes, hours or days afterward.

Here is an incendiary pencil undergoing a bench test. The size and energy of the flame indicate the amount of damage it could do.

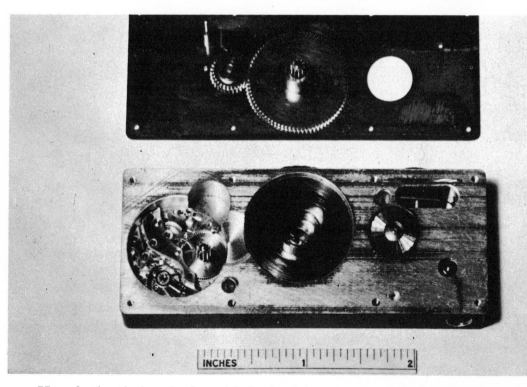

Here is the timing device with its back cover removed, showing the large coiled driving spring. The clock is only four inches long.

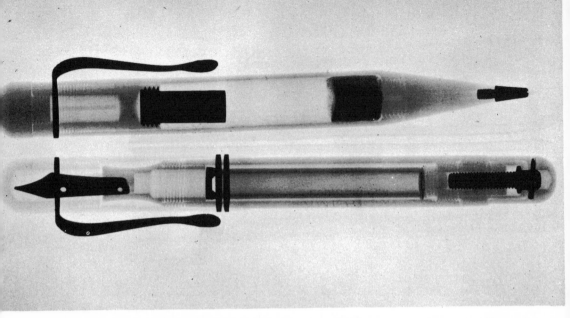

This X-ray photograph shows an incendiary pen and pencil set in its carrying case, as the German saboteurs brought them over.

They also were equipped with demolition blocks of TNT, wrapped in paper. These parcels of destruction weighed about two pounds.

The pen and pencil assembled for use as a delayed-action device. The two caps and the pencil point form no part of this incendiary.

Here is one of the blocks of TNT. The hole in the end accommodates a detonator. The scrapings were made by the FBI for analysis.

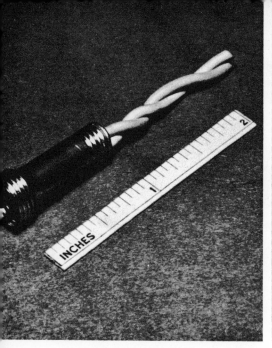 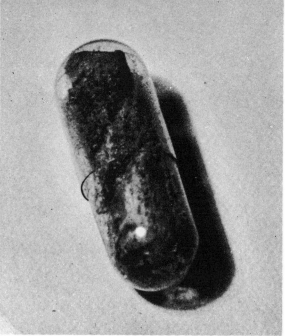

German incendiary devices were tiny and ingenious. Left, an electric match; right, fire materials contained in medicinal capsules.

 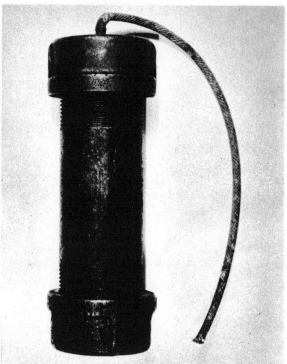

The 13-jewel watch mechanism at left was contained in a timing device. At right, a "pineapple," a crude bomb made of steel pipe.

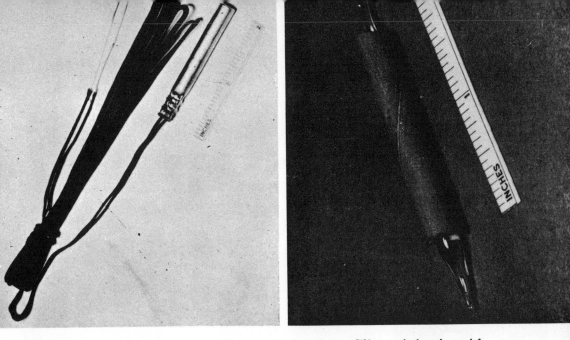

This electric blasting cap is only two inches long. The sulphuric acid capsule at right is encased in rubber tubing.

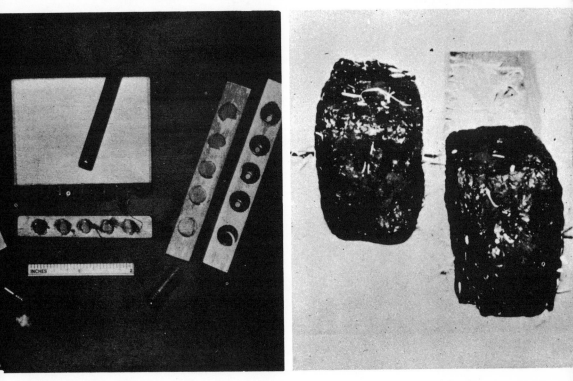

Detonators were brought over concealed in small wooden blocks; TNT was disguised as lumps of coal for use in plants and factories.

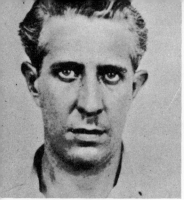

Richard Quirin
Death

Herbert Hans Haupt
Death

Ernest P. Burger
Life Term

Hermann Neubauer
Death

Carl Reuper
16 Years

George John Dasch
30 Years

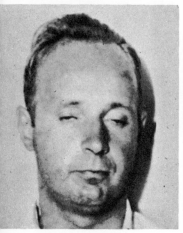

Erich Strunck
10 Years

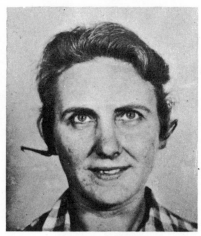

Else Weustenfeld
5 Years

Werner Thiel
Death

The eight saboteurs and some of the spies in the Duquesne ring,
248

Everett Roeder
16 Years

Rene Mezenen
8 Years

Axel Wheeler-Hill
15 Years

Paul Scholz
16 Years

Heinrich Harm Heinck
Death

Edward Kerling
Death

Heinrich Clausing
8 Years

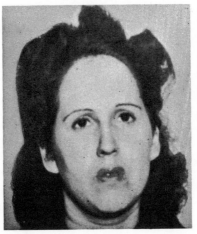
Lilly Stein
10 Years

Herman Lang
18 Years

and the sentences they drew when convicted on the FBI's charges.

249

The Postwar Period

 T HE FBI has learned through the years that no sooner is one emergency met and overcome than another arises. This is particularly true today. After thwarting the greatest threat to the internal security of the United States that the country has ever faced the Bureau found itself confronted with a crime wave of serious proportions and an even more insidious threat to the Nation's internal security—the menace of Communism.

Murders, armed robberies, bank holdups, and rapes once more blackened the front pages of the nation's newspapers. The estimated number of major crimes for 1947 amounted to 1,665,110. Crime has continued to march upward through the years as the number of serious crimes has increased from 1,686,670 in 1948, 1,763,290 in 1949, 1,790,030 in 1950, 1,882,160 in 1951 to 2,036,510 in 1952, an 8.2 per cent increase over the previous year. Estimated serious crimes for 1953 totaled 2,159,080, an increase of 6 per cent over 1952.

The year 1952 is very significant for it is the first calendar year during which the number of estimated serious crimes in the United States has exceeded the two million mark. Equally significant is the year 1953 for the number of serious crimes during that year also surpassed two million. During each 24-hour period in 1953, 173 persons were robbed, 1,313 burglaries were reported to the police, 621 cars were stolen in addition to 3,471 miscellaneous larcenies of various types having been committed. There were also 35 felonious homicides and 254 aggravated assaults committed each day. Every 14.6 seconds during 1953, a serious crime was committed.

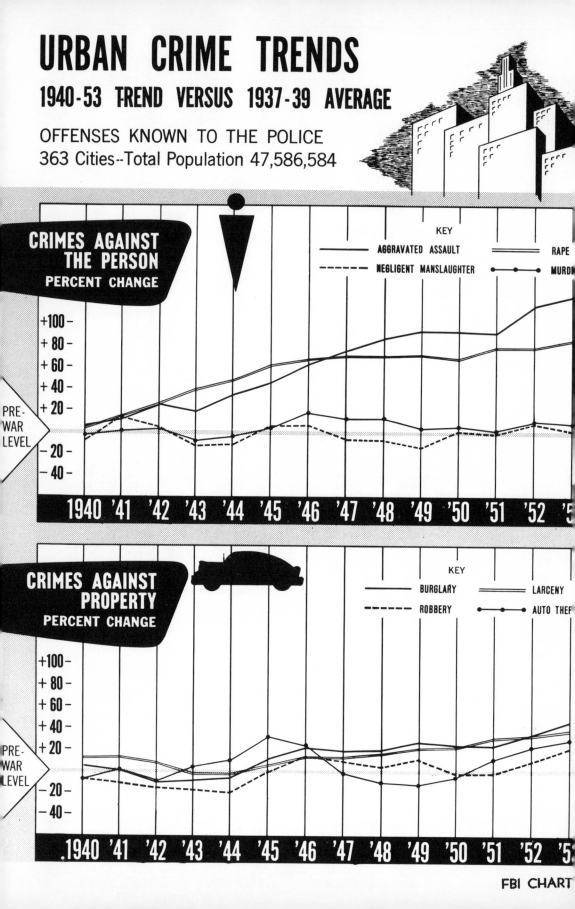

URBAN CRIME TRENDS

1940-53 TREND VERSUS 1937-39 AVERAGE

OFFENSES KNOWN TO THE POLICE
363 Cities--Total Population 47,586,584

CRIMES AGAINST THE PERSON
PERCENT CHANGE

KEY
- AGGRAVATED ASSAULT
- NEGLIGENT MANSLAUGHTER
- RAPE
- MURD[ER]

+100 —
+ 80 —
+ 60 —
+ 40 —
+ 20 —
PRE-WAR LEVEL
— 20 —
— 40 —

1940 '41 '42 '43 '44 '45 '46 '47 '48 '49 '50 '51 '52 '5[3]

CRIMES AGAINST PROPERTY
PERCENT CHANGE

KEY
- BURGLARY
- LARCENY
- ROBBERY
- AUTO THEF[T]

+100 —
+ 80 —
+ 60 —
+ 40 —
+ 20 —
PRE-WAR LEVEL
— 20 —
— 40 —

.1940 '41 '42 '43 '44 '45 '46 '47 '48 '49 '50 '51 '52 '5[3]

FBI CHART

The analysis of fingerprint arrest cards received in FBI Identification Division during the postwar period verified the fact that a substantial portion of the crime committed was attributable to persons under voting age. In 1948 there were 115,940 persons under the age of twenty-one who were arrested and fingerprinted, this number constituting 15.3 per cent of the total arrests during this period. This number rose to 117,562 in 1949, 118,426 in 1950 and 119,676 in 1951.

What are the causes of this increase in crimes committed by youthful offenders? Why are youthful gangs found roaming the streets of the large metropolitan centers and operating even in rural communities? In nearly every investigation of juvenile crime, it has been found that a delinquent adult contributed to the delinquency of the young offender through example, laxity, poor home management, derelict training or failure to discharge his responsibilities. These causes appear regularly in investigations to determine why youngsters become delinquent: broken homes (resulting from death or divorce), neglectful parents, immorality in the home, lack of religion, improper discipline, untrained parents, failure to support the disciplinary efforts of teachers, poverty.

All of these conditions flourished and were exaggerated by the stresses of war; therefore, it is not hard to understand what went wrong with our young people. During war years, the criminal tendencies of juveniles took an upward spurt because their elders were too busy with other matters to provide necessary supervision. Fathers were in the armed services, mothers were in war plants, homes were disrupted, the excitement of war's alarms upset normal living conditions, police and social agencies were too occupied with what seemed to be more pressing affairs to attend to youth's needs, and money came to them too easily. Teen-age hoodlumism flourished; the dive, the corner hangout became spawning beds of crime, and shortly these youngsters were launched on a criminal career.

What is to be done about it? The FBI and local police forces cannot handle the situation alone. They need the help of every law-abiding citizen. FBI records reveal that the home is the most important factor in the prevention of juvenile delinquency. It must be closely supported by the churches, schools, law enforcement agencies, civic and fraternal groups. It has been found that the amount of crime in a given locality may be inversely compared with the efficiency of the municipal government and its interest in the development of good citizenship. Thus the cure is in the hands of the people themselves.

*Using fire escape of an evacuated New York house as headquarters,
children play a dangerously realistic game of guerrilla warfare.*

254

In Cleveland an abandoned precinct station was made into "boystown" headquarters. Here youths are removing old cell blocks.

PERSONS ARRESTED UNDER 18 YEARS OF AGE

PERCENT OF TOTAL ARRESTS
Crimes Against Property
1,174 CITIES--TOTAL POPULATION 37,255,808

CALENDAR YEAR 1953

OFFENSES	● UNDER 18	TOTAL ARRES ALL AG
Robbery	18.0%	11,786
Burglary	49.3%	36,879
Larceny	40.1%	68,195
Auto Theft	53.6%	20,391
Embezzlement and Fraud	3.6%	11,877
Receiving Stolen Property	24.9%	2,734
Forgery and Counterfeiting	6.6%	7,151

CHART

In March, 1950, Mr. Hoover inaugurated the "Ten Most Wanted Fugitives" program as a practical investigative technique to effect the location and apprehension of fugitives badly wanted by the FBI. The program affords nationwide publicity to these dangerous criminals by a widespread and continuous distribution of their photographs, together with graphic accounts of their criminal activities. From the inception of the program in March, 1950, through August 23, 1954, no less than 70 of these menacing criminals were brought to justice. Of this number, the arrests of 31 fugitives could be directly attributed to observant and co-operative citizens who recognized pictures or descriptive data publicized throughout the nation in connection with this program.

The list of Ten Most Wanted Fugitives is composed of criminals badly wanted by the FBI for the perpetration of one or more of the Federal violations within the investigative jurisdiction of the FBI. The selection of the fugitives who appear on this list is based upon the composite evaluation of past criminal record, viciousness, national interest, widespread activity and potential menace to society. As each fugitive is eliminated from the list through his apprehension another is added.

During the era of the "roaring 30's" organized gangs of criminals were flourishing and prospering in the United States. The apprehension of the leaders of these gangs such as John Dillinger, Alvin Karpis, "Ma" Barker, "Pretty Boy" Floyd or "Machine Gun" Kelly usually led to the arrest and conviction of numerous accomplices. Such is not the case today, however, because effective law enforcement has prevented the successful organization of criminal gangs. Individuals whose names appear on today's Ten Most Wanted Fugitives list are not of organized gangs but, in the main, are individually acting desperadoes.

The capture of one of the early additions to the FBI's list of Ten Most Wanted Fugitives, at St. Paul, Minnesota, in 1950, affords an excellent example of the assistance that citizens, youths as well as adults, can render to law enforcement agencies. Two boys, aged 13 and 14, observed the man's photograph in their local newspaper and believed him to be identical with a man then living in a cave on the edge of the city of St. Paul. The youths notified the

St. Paul Police Department which sent officers to the scene and took him into custody.

The local newspaper rewarded the boys with a trip to Washington, D. C., and while they were in the nation's capital, Mr. Hoover personally conveyed his congratulations to the youths for their alertness. Thus, by joining together the ranks of law enforcement with public-spirited citizens in the nation, the Ten Most Wanted Fugitives program has proved to be an effective weapon in the endless battle against crime.

Ten Most Wanted Fugitives exhibit in FBI headquarters at Washington after the addition, on July 27, 1953, of George William Krendich to this list.

From time to time the cry has been raised that the solution to the crime problem rests in the establishment of a national police force whose authority would extend to every nook and cranny of the United States. Such a force would take over the duties which have always been designated to the local, county, and state agencies. This Federal police organization would then be all-powerful in the law enforcement field and would undertake the suppression of crime on a nationwide basis. Mr. Hoover has always disagreed with such a proposal and has stated over the years that crime is primarily a local problem. He sees in a Federal police agency a positive danger to the inherent freedoms and liberties of the American people and a marked departure from constitutional government in this country. The Federal Government, he points out, can never be a satisfactory substitute for local self-government in the law enforcement field. The present system, despite certain shortcomings and weaknesses, is the approach to the crime problem with the responsibility for suppressing crime resting on established local authorities in the various communities where crimes are being committed. The role of the Federal Government must continue to be one of lending assistance to local agencies co-operating with them in matters of mutual interest and encouraging them to work with one another. The FBI for many years has been lending assistance to local law enforcement agencies in the field of police training. It has also made available to these agencies the facilities of the vast fingerprint files of the FBI as well as the FBI Laboratory.

For the past two decades, the FBI has been active in the training of local, county, and state law enforcement officers as well as other Federal law enforcing agencies. The FBI National Academy which was established in July, 1935, by Mr. Hoover was a pioneering step in the field of law enforcement training. Approximately eighty officers from local, state, and Federal agencies attend each of the two sessions of the Academy held annually. Designed to train officers as instructors and administrators in their local departments, the National Academy provides instruction in more than one hundred subjects dealing with various aspects of the law enforcement profession. There is no charge either to the officer or to the law enforcement agency he is representing for the instruction provided by the FBI. Those attending the National Academy do, however, pay their own living expenses while they are attending the Academy.

The Honorable Earl Warren, Chief Justice of the United States, delivering his address at the graduation exercises of the 52nd Session of the FBI National Academy on November 20, 1953, in the Departmental Auditorium, Washington, D. C.

The facilities of the FBI in Washington and also at the FBI training facilities on the Marine Base at Quantico, Virginia, are used by the National Academy. With the graduation of the Fifty-third Session of the Academy on June 11, 1954, a total of 2,826 officers representing law enforcement agencies in all parts of the nation and in territorial possessions have been graduated. More than one hundred thousand law enforcement officers have received the benefits of the training received by these graduates.

The training the National Academy men undergo is rugged and intensive. Those attending the Academy must be less than fifty-one years of age and must be in good physical condition to enable them to study and work from early morning to late at night. To watch the officers for a few days on the ranges at Quantico is a revelation of the benefits they derive at the hands of FBI instructors. All of them have carried a revolver for years yet some have never had the occasion to fire at a criminal. At first some are slow and clumsy with their weapons and bullets are inclined to miss the target as often as they hit it. Most of them have had little training in safety rules and the handling of weapons for the simple reason that their departments can't afford to pay for ammunition for regular practice. After a few days on the range their scores begin to rise. The officers gain new confidence in their ability. They have little difficulty in hitting the targets, and they begin to realize that when they go home their communities are going to be better protected.

Since the inauguration of the FBI Academy in 1935, Mr. Hoover has received innumerable letters from graduates of the Academy expressing their appreciation for having had the opportunity to attend. Some letters from these officers have related the details of gun battles they have had with criminals and attribute the fact they are alive today to the excellent firearms instruction they received while attending the National Academy.

The FBI also provides co-operation in training programs of local police departments in all parts of the United States. Assigned to each of the FBI's fifty-two field offices are Special Agents who have been trained as police instructors. State, county, and municipal law enforcement agencies may request FBI co-operation in the training programs which they carry on in their respective departments. In addition to instructing the local officers, these Special

261

Agents assist in planning curriculums which will best meet the training needs of individual departments. During the 1954 fiscal year the FBI co-operated upon request in 2,662 police training schools.

In many instances, the FBI takes the initiative in the inauguration of training programs designed to combat certain crimes. For example, after noting the general increase of automobile thefts throughout the United States, the FBI sponsored a series of 131 law enforcement auto theft conferences throughout the United States during 1952 and 1953. The purpose of these conferences was to discuss the problem of auto thefts and to promote a mutual exchange of ideas. More than eight thousand persons attended these conferences on auto thefts. FBI law enforcement conferences on thefts from interstate shipments began in April, 1953, and 133 of these conferences were held during that year. Another series of such conferences devoted to interstate transportation of stolen property violations began early in 1954.

In its participation in training programs of law enforcement agencies, the FBI has continually emphasized the adoption and development of the highest personal and ethical standards. It has continually directed its efforts toward strengthening America's defense against crime and developing a warm expression of co-operation within the law enforcement profession. The products of this co-operative spirit are seen in the improved techniques and greater resources which are now available to all agencies regardless of their size or geographic location.

As a service agency to law enforcement, the FBI makes perhaps its greatest contribution through its Identification Division. Founded on the scientific premise that the fingerprint impressions of no two human beings are identical, the fingerprint files have astounded all who have ever seen them. The Identification Division was created in 1924 as a national clearing house for criminal arrest data through the efforts of Director Hoover and the International Association of Chiefs of Police. The fingerprint collections maintained by the IACP and the Federal Penitentiary at Leavenworth, Kansas, a total of 810,188 fingerprints were turned over to he FBI. Today there are more than 131,000,000 sets of fingerprints on file and each working day approximately twenty thousand fingerprint cards are received for processing. Immediately upon receipt, fingerprints of arrested persons are searched through the fingerprint files and a complete identification record is sent to the contributing agency.

A general view of the building housing the FBI Identification Division, Washington, D. C.

Fingerprints pour in at the rate of more than 20,000 daily. Above, prints are being prepared for introduction as evidence in the courtroom.

A portion of the criminal fingerprint files in the FBI Identification Division, Washington, D. C.

An expert in the single fingerprint section of the FBI Identification Division, Washington, D. C., is shown dusting an automatic for latent fingerprints.

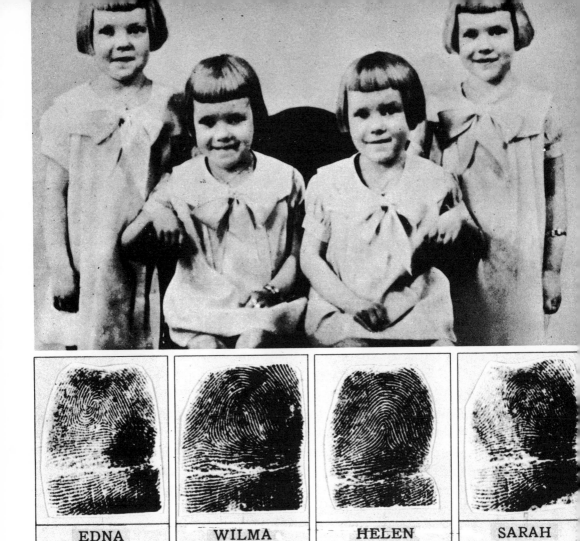

| EDNA | WILMA | HELEN | SARAH |

Fingerprints remain unchanged during the life of an individual. The ridges remain constant, although they may be affected by deep cuts or burns, or rendered indistinct for a time by occupational activity like plaster work or dishwashing. But this effacement is only temporary, and the ridges resume their former outlines shortly after such work ceases. No two fingers have ever been found with identical patterns. The picture above shows that the characteristics of the Morlock quadruplets are very similar. Their fingerprints, however, are entirely different. No two of the finger impressions of the girls are identical; even the classifications of their prints are dissimilar. The corresponding impressions of the fingers of Edna and Sarah are of the same pattern, but the four prints clearly show the individuality of the characteristics.

265

Not all of the fingerprint cards received by the FBI reflect arrests on criminal charges. The majority of the fingerprint cards, representing over sixty million persons in the United States, are of the noncriminal variety and include fingerprint cards for aliens, government employees, armed services, and personal identification. The twenty-six and one-half million criminal fingerprint cards represent approximately ten million different persons in the United States.

The existence of fingerprint cards in the FBI files for personal identification purposes has been helpful in identifying unknown dead and amnesia victims. A few months ago the police department of a large metropolitan city supervised the burial of an unknown man in potter's field after all attempts to establish the identity of the deceased had failed. This being the customary interment in such cases, little public notice would have been taken of the proceedings except for one singular fact — it was the first time in ten years that the police of that city had been unable to obtain an identification of a deceased person. A human tragedy once quite common-place had now become a rarity. Identifications of unknown dead are made so frequently in the Identification Division of the FBI that this work is now considered one of the standard services to other law enforcement agencies. Like many other forms of police service, identification of the dead is routine work which seldom comes to public attention.

Another example of the co-operation afforded local law enforcement agencies is the FBI Laboratory which was established in 1932. Today the services of skilled crime laboratory technicians are no farther from any American law enforcement agency than the nearest post office or express depot. The FBI Laboratory conducts examinations of criminal evidence submitted by law enforcement agencies throughout the United States. The vast facilities of the Laboratory are thus available to even the smallest law enforcement agencies consisting of only one or two employees. The examiners in the Laboratory are also available to testify in court concerning the examinations they have conducted. The initial examinations and the subsequent testimony of the examiner at the scene of the trial are cost-free services available to these law enforcement agencies. Mr. Hoover established the Laboratory because he felt the scientific approach to crime detection and investigation was the most logical approach. The latest scientific instruments, including the electron microscope and the infra-red spectrophotometer, have been obtained and are constantly used in Laboratory examinations. The growth of the Laboratory and the successful application of scientific crime detection have resulted in the solution of many crimes that would otherwise have been unsolved.

The *FBI Law Enforcement Bulletin,* published monthly by the FBI for distribution to law enforcement agencies in all parts of the nation, regularly includes improvements and new developments in the field of law enforcement. The FBI has become a clearing house of information concerning new ideas and new techniques valuable to those in the law enforcement profession which are made available to them through this monthly publication.

The Congress of the United States passed a law during 1866 making it a Federal offense to deprive an individual of certain rights and privileges granted by the Constitution and the laws of the United States. Investigations of alleged violations of this law, commonly referred to as civil rights cases, are under the investigative jurisdiction of the FBI.

The protection of civil rights is one of the basic functions of law enforcement. Any destruction of an individual's civil rights is a crime, subject to prosecution under existing statutes. Civil rights investigations are considered by the FBI as cases of major importance and are afforded prompt and thorough attention; however, it is the policy of the FBI to conduct complete investigations of alleged violations of civil rights only when instructed to do so by the Department of Justice.

When initiating civil rights investigations it is the policy of the FBI to notify the head of the agency or institution involved, and who is advised of the nature of the allegation and that the FBI has been instructed to make an investigation. Any state or local investigations that have previously been made concerning the allegation may be brought to the FBI's attention at this time. Between Jan. 1, 1948 and June 30, 1954 the FBI instituted investigations of more than 5,600 alleged violations under the Civil Rights statutes.

Instead of leveling off as might have been expected following the cessation of World War II, the FBI's work steadily increased as a result of legislation and executive orders which placed new investigative responsibilities upon it. This was due primarily to the sinister danger to the security of the country — the threat posed by the Communist party, USA, its followers and sympathizers. The vacancy created by the defeat of Nazism and Fascism was quickly filled by Red Fascism. Most important were the Atomic Energy Act of 1946 and the Federal Employees Loyalty Program.

The Atomic Energy Act of August 1, 1946, gave the FBI the responsibility of determining the character, associates, and loyalty of individuals employed by the Atomic Energy Commission and all other individuals having access to restricted atomic energy data. The principal objective of the investigation under this Act is to determine if the individual being investigated may be or would constitute a hazard to the security of the secret and restricted data concerning atomic energy.

During the 1952 fiscal year, the FBI received a total of 89,689 requests for investigations under the Atomic Energy Act as amended. Investigative reports in these cases were furnished to the Atomic Energy Commission, and the FBI, in accordance with long-established policy, made no recommendations concerning action to be taken.

Because of the tremendous work load being handled by the FBI, Congress relieved it of certain routine applicant type investigations by passage of Public Law 298 which went into effect October 2, 1952. This law substituted the Civil Service Commission as the investigative agency to handle routine Atomic Energy Act applicant cases. As a result, applicant cases received by the FBI for investigation under the Atomic Energy Act were reduced to 45,693 and 25,732 for the fiscal years 1953 and 1954 respectively.

The Federal Employees Loyalty Program based on Executive Order 9835 became effective August 1, 1947. Under this program the FBI was required to search through its files the names and fingerprints of all employees and applicants for positions in the executive branch of the Government. When derogatory information was located concerning the loyalty of an individual, preliminary inquiries were made and many full field investigations were conducted to confirm or determine the exact significance of information obtained from the initial search of FBI files. Copies of reports in these cases were made available to the Civil Service Commission for appropriate action.

This program was changed to the Federal Employees Security Program by Executive Order 10450 which became effective on May 28, 1953. This executive order not only takes cognizance of the loyalty of Government employees, but considers drunkenness, dope addiction, nervous or mental disorders, sex deviation, et cetera, as factors to be considered when determining whether or not an individual is a security risk.

The reports in these cases are submitted to the Civil Service Commission without conclusions or recommendations. It is the responsibility of the employing agency to weigh the facts and to determine the proper administrative action. By the close of the 1953 fiscal year 4,772,278 loyalty or security forms had been processed; 27,200 preliminary inquiries had been initiated; and 27,326 full field investigations had been conducted.

On the basis of these investigations the Civil Service Commission reported that as of May 28, 1953, 557 persons had been dismissed or denied employment; 6,382 persons had left Government service or had withdrawn from consideration for employment during the investigation or before their cases had been adjudicated.

The former Attorney General, Francis Biddle, as far back as May 28, 1942, found that the Communist party from the time of its inception in 1919 believed in, advised, advocated, and taught the overthrow of the Government of the United States by force and violence. In 1944, the party allegedly dissolved and changed its name to "The Communist Political Association." During the war years and while the United States and Soviet Russia were allies, the Communist party and the Communist Political Association supported the war effort against the common enemy. This bit of deception on the part of the Communists was short-lived, however, for shortly after a blast by a French Communist leader, Jacques Duclos, the Communist Political Association was quickly

Below are shown freak handguns occasionally encountered by Agents in their work. Left to right they are a four-barrel pistol, a .41-caliber

double-barrel derringer, a .32-caliber cylindrical revolver, and a .25-caliber four-barrel pistol of French manufacture.

This tiny camera, easily concealed in the hand, enables a Special Agent to take photographs of suspected persons unobtrusively.

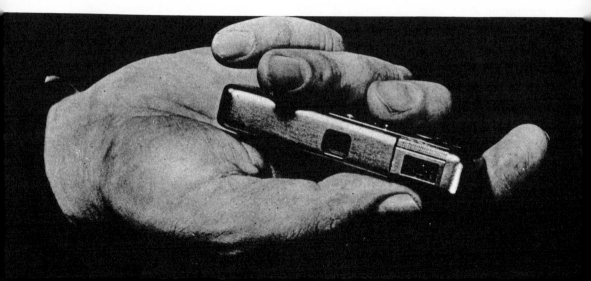

relegated to oblivion. In July, 1945, the Communist party was re-established; its old policies of disruption and perfidy were again publicly proclaimed and promoted by its leaders.

In 1948, twelve members of the National Board of the Communist party were arrested and charged with violation of the Smith Act which makes conspiracy to teach and advocate the overthrow and destruction of the United States Government by force and violence a Federal offense. After their conviction (eleven were convicted — one was severed from the trial) in 1949, the Communist party leaders appealed their case to the Supreme Court of the United States which upheld the constitutionality of the Smith Act under which they were convicted. On the basis of this action taken by the Supreme Court, the Department of Justice and the FBI took prosecutive action against additional leaders of the Communist party. From 1948, when the national leaders of the Communist party were arrested, through August 15, 1954, 120 Communist leaders had been indicted by Federal Grand Juries for violation of the Smith Act. All but one of the indictments charged these individuals with conspiracy to teach and advocate the overthrow and destruction of the United States Government by force and violence. Of the 84 who had been tried by August 15, 1954, 81 were found guilty; 3 were acquitted; and 6 severed due to ill health or death. Sentences for those found guilty and sentenced, totaled 311 years and $421,000 in fines.

In January, 1947, the membership of the Communist party in the United States was approximately 74,000. The estimated number was reduced to 43,000 in January 1951, and as of June, 1953, the estimated membership of the Communist party in the United States was less than 25,000. The spotlight of aroused public opinion and the successful prosecution of Communist party functionaries have dealt the party a damaging blow. We must remember, however, that the strength of the party cannot be determined by the number of its members. Membership of the party today is composed largely of disciplined and trusted "hard core" members who can be depended upon to carry out any assignment. They have invoked strict security measures to make the Bureau's efforts to obtain legal evidence concerning their activities more difficult. Membership cards are no longer carried, few records are kept, and much of their energy recently has been devoted to perfecting their underground organization. Members of the underground frequently alter

271

their physical appearance and personal habits, desert their families and move suddenly to different localities. Keeping track of their underground activities requires the constant devising of new investigative techniques and the increasing use of specially trained personnel.

Even while the United States and Russia were fighting together as allies during World War II, Soviet espionage agents were operating in this country. Their primary target was America's progress in the development of the atomic bomb. After it was determined that the secrets of atomic bomb construction had been acquired by a foreign power, it was the FBI's responsibility to find the individuals responsible. Every resource of the FBI was directed toward this objective. This investigation led to Dr. Klaus Fuchs, former German Communist and later a British scientist who was in the United States as a member of a British scientific mission. It was determined that Fuchs' contact in the United States was Harry Gold, a chemical engineer who delivered to the Soviets information obtained by Fuchs. Gold was sentenced to 30 years' imprisonment on December 9, 1950, for his part in the theft of atomic secrets from the United States.

Another espionage case involved Julius and Ethel Rosenberg, both of whom had been members of the Communist party. They were tried, convicted, and sentenced to death for violations of the espionage statutes. The Rosenbergs were executed at Sing Sing Prison, Ossining, New York, on June 19, 1953. Much of the Communist party propaganda activity during 1952 and 1953 was based upon the Rosenberg case.

Since the end of the war the investigation of the Soviet espionage apparatus in this country has been one of the FBI's principal pursuits. The results of. FBI activities in this field cannot be measured entirely in terms of the number of persons convicted or sentences imposed. In many cases it is more important to identify an espionage agent and permit him to continue his operations under close observation than immediately to take him into custody for prosecutive action. Through such operations the Government is able to ascertain the full ramifications and activities of the apparatus to which he is attached.

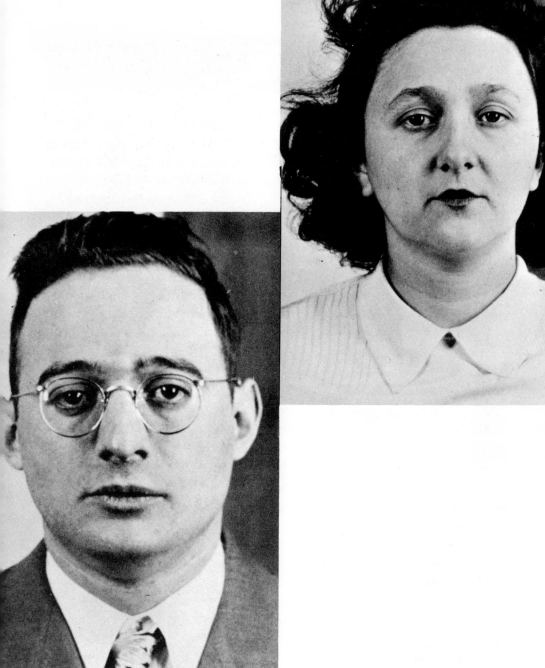

Julius and Ethel Rosenberg, arrested by FBI Agents July 17 and August 11, 1950 respectively, for conspiracy to commit espionage. Tried, convicted, and sentenced to death on April 5, 1951, they were executed at Sing Sing Prison, June 19, 1953.

Robert George Thompson, former National Communist Party Board member, who was arrested by FBI Agents at Twain Harte, California, on August 27, 1953. While Thompson was a fugitive he dyed his hair and eyebrows, grew a mustache, and gained thirty pounds.

CRIME FREQUENCY IN THE UNITED STATES

	One case every
Larceny	24.9 seconds
Burglary	1.1 minutes
Auto theft	2.3 minutes
Assault	5.7 minutes
Robbery	8.3 minutes
Rape	29.4 minutes
Murder and Manslaughter	73.8 minutes
Manslaughter (negligent)	92.4 minutes

Figures based on averages of such crimes
in the U. S. for 1953.

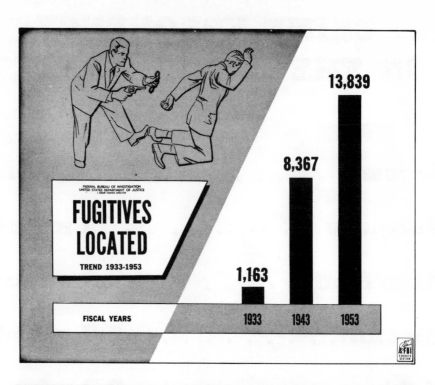

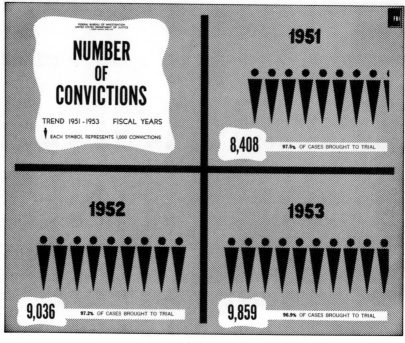

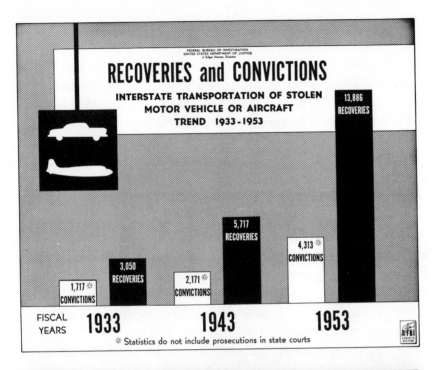

FEDERAL BUREAU OF INVESTIGATION
UNITED STATES DEPARTMENT OF JUSTICE
J. Edgar Hoover, Director

RECOVERIES and CONVICTIONS

INTERSTATE TRANSPORTATION OF STOLEN
MOTOR VEHICLE OR AIRCRAFT
TREND 1933-1953

13,886 RECOVERIES

5,717 RECOVERIES

4,313 ⁎ CONVICTIONS

3,050 RECOVERIES

2,171 ⁎ CONVICTIONS

1,717 ⁎ CONVICTIONS

FISCAL YEARS   1933   1943   1953

⁎ Statistics do not include prosecutions in state courts

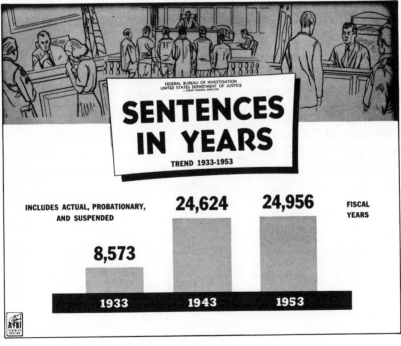

FEDERAL BUREAU OF INVESTIGATION
UNITED STATES DEPARTMENT OF JUSTICE
J. EDGAR HOOVER, DIRECTOR

SENTENCES IN YEARS

TREND 1933-1953

INCLUDES ACTUAL, PROBATIONARY,
AND SUSPENDED

24,624   24,956   FISCAL YEARS

8,573

1933   1943   1953

The internal security of the United Sates can be assured with the co-operation, aid, and assistance of every law-abiding person in our nation. Plans have already been made and are in operation whereby the law enforcement agencies of the nation are working in close co-operation with the FBI.

Individuals and patriotic citizens can best serve the FBI and the nation by being alert and furnishing all pertinent facts in their possession to the FBI, which is as near to everyone as his telephone. The FBI is interested in receiving facts and is desirous of avoiding malicious gossip or idle rumors. Citizens who have furnished information to the FBI should not draw conclusions since the data they possess might be incomplete or only partially accurate.

Once the information has been reported to the FBI, you should never endeavor to make private investigations. This can best be done by trained investigators who have access to data acquired over the years on individuals engaged in subversive activities. Hysteria, witch-hunts, and vigilantes weaken internal security. Internal security investigations require care and painstaking effort. We can all contribute to our internal security by protecting the innocent as well as by identifying the enemies within our midst.

The individuals most anxious to weaken our internal security are not always easy to identify; however, the Communist party line is clear. Its first concern is the advancement of Soviet Russia and the godless Communist cause. It is important that we learn to know the enemies of the American way of life.

Co-operative individuals willing to furnish information can help the FBI a great deal. You can be certain that the FBI will be on the job twenty-four hours a day, year in and year out, living up to its tradition of fidelity, bravery, integrity. With J. Edgar Hoover as Director of the FBI, the public may be assured that the Bureau will continue, as in the past, to respond to the needs of American citizens.

Picture Credits

Index